mean cheap necessarily. Food lovers know the difference between a restaurant where the high prices are fully justified by the quality of the ingredients and the excellence of the cooking and presentation of the food, and meretricious establishments where high prices are merely the result of pretentious attitudes.

Some of the restaurants featured here are undeniably expensive if you consume caviar and champagne, but even haute cuisine establishments offer set-price menus (especially at lunchtime) allowing budget diners to enjoy dishes created by top chefs and every bit as good as those on the regular menu. At the same time, some of the eating places listed here might not make it into more conventional food guides, because they are relatively humble cafés or takeaways. Some are deliberately oriented towards tourists, but there is nothing wrong in that: what some guides dismiss as 'tourist traps' may be deservedly popular for providing choice and good value.

FEEDBACK

You may or may not agree with the author's choice – in either case we would like to know about your experiences. Any feedback you give us and any recommendations you make will be followed up, so that you can look forward to seeing your restaurant suggestions in print in the next edition.

Feedback forms have been included at the back of the book and you can e-mail us with comments by writing to: *timeforfood@thomascook.com*. No food guide can keep pace with the changing restaurant scene, as chefs move on, establishments open or close, and menus, opening hours or credit card details change. Let us know what you like or do not like about the restaurants featured here. Tell us if you discover shops, pubs, cafés, bars, restaurants or markets that

you think should go in the guide. Let us know if you discover changes – say to telephone numbers or opening times.

Symbols used in this guide

VISA	Visa accepted
⓪	Diners Club accepted
ⓜ	MasterCard accepted
🍴	Restaurant
🍷	Bar, café or pub
🧺	Shop, market or picnic site
✆	Telephone
ⓣ	Transport
❷	Numbered red circles relate to the maps at the start of the section

The price indications used in this guide have the following meanings:

€	budget level
€€	typical/average for the destination
€€€	up-market

Introduction | 3

FOOD FINDER

RESTAURANTS A–Z

A
L'Affriolé 48
Alcazar 39
Alain Ducasse 58
Allard 39
L'Alsaco 68
Altitude 95 57, 76
L'Ambassade d'Auvergne 19
Les Ambassadeurs 58
L'Ambroisie 19
L'Arpège 48
À Sousceyrac 79
Au C'Amelot 79
Au Pied de Cochon 8
Aux Charpentiers 39

B
Les Bacchantes 68
Le Balzar 28
La Bamboche 49
Le Bar au Sel 49
La Bastide Odéon 40
Benoit 19
Bistro Romain 56
Bofinger 19
Les Bouchons de François Clerc 87
Les Bookinistes 41
Le Bourdonnais 49
Brasserie de L'Île St-Louis 20
Le Buisson Ardent 28
Burger King 57

C
Le Carré des Feuillants 8
La Casserole 17
Le Cave Drouot 68
Chez Catherine 69
Chez Henri au Moulin à Vent 28
Chez Jean 69
Chez Joël D – Bistro de l'Huître 29
Chez Michel 77, 79
Chez Paul 79
Chez René 29
Chez Vong 16
Chicago Meatpackers 57
Le Cinq 60
La Closerie des Lilas 41
Le Convivial 69
Il Cortile 10
Le Coupe-Chou 29

D
Le Divellec 49

E
Écaille et Plume 51
Les Élyssées du Vernet 66
L'Épi Dupin 41
L'Espadon 10
L'Étoile du Kashmir 79

F
Les Fontaines 31

G
La Galoche d'Aurilliac 80
La Gazelle 17
Gérard Besson 10
Gli Angeli 20
Le Grand Véfour 11
Le Grizzli 20
La Guirlande de Julie 20
Guy Savoy 60, 66

H
Hard Rock Café 57, 66, 73
Hippo 56

I
Isse 11

J
Jacques Cagna 41
Le Jardin 60
Jo Goldenberg 21
Jules Verne 51, 76
Les Jumeaux 80
Justine 57

L
Lapérouse 41, 66, 67
Laurent 61

M
Maxim's 61
McDonald's 57
Mirama 31
Le Moulin à Vins 70

N
New Nioulaville 16

P
Le Pactole 31
Paul Minchelli 51
Pharamond 66, 67
Pierre Gagnaire 61
Pile ou Face 11
Planet Hollywood 66
Le Poquelin 11
Le Président 16

R
Le Relais Louis XIII 41
Le Restaurant de l'Astor 61
Restaurant Opéra 70
Restaurant du Palais-Royal 11
Le Roi du Pot au Feu 70

S
Spoon, Food and Wine 61

T
Taillevent 66
La Tour d'Argent 31, 66
Le Train Bleu 77

V
La Verrière 71
Le Vieux Bistro 21
Le Villaret 81
La Ville de Jagannath 81
Le Violon d'Ingres 51

W, Z
Woolloomooloo 17
La Zygotissoire 81

BARS, CAFÉS AND PUBS A–Z

A
L'Aréa 22
L'Armagnac 82
L'Assignat 42
Au Général Lafayette 72
Au P'tit Creux du Faubourg 72
Au Sauvignon 52
The Auld Alliance 22
Aux Négociants 77

B
Le Bar Bat 82
Bar de l'Entr'acte 12
Bar des Théatres 62
Barfly 62
Le Baron Bouge 82
The Bowler 62
Brasserie Lipp 42
Bugsy's 62

C
Le Café 12
Café-Bar le Nemours 12
Café Beaubourg 22
Café Charbon 82
Café le Dôme 52
Café de Flore 42
Café des Hauteurs 52
Café des Lettres 52
Café Madeleine 62
Café de la Mairie 42
Café du Marché 52
Le Café Marly 76
Café des Musées 22
Café de la Paix 72
Le Café du Passage 82
Café des Phares 23
Café de la Poste 32
Café Thoumieux 52
Café du Trésor 23
Le Café Zephyr 72
Les Caves de Bourgogne 32
Chez Georges 43
Chez Karine 23
La Chope 32
Clown Bar 83
Le Cochon à l'Oreille 12
Colette 12
Le Comptoir de Relais 43
The Cricketer 62

D
Les Deux Magots 43

E
L'Écluse 43
L'Entract 72

F
Flowers Café 32
Le Fouquet's 63
La Fourmi 73

G
La Gueuze 33

H
Hard Rock Café 73
Harry's Bar 13
Hemingway Bar 13

J
Jacques Mélac 83, 86
Juveniles 13, 87

L
Le Lutétia 43

M
Master's Bar 53
Le Mauzac 33
Le Mecano Bar 83
Montecristo Café 63
Le Mouffetard 33

P
La Palette 43
Le Passage 83

R
Le Rallye 33
Le Reflet 33
Le Rouquet 53

S
Sancerre 53

T
Tabac de la Sorbonne 33

V
Villa Barclay 63
Virgin Café 63

W
Web Bar 23
Willi's Wine Bar 13, 87

SHOPS A–Z
À La Mère de Famille 74
À La Petite Fabrique 84
Albert Menes 64
L'Ambassade du Sud-Ouest 54
André Cleret 14

Androuet 54
Au Levain du Marais 24
Au Panetier 14
Barthélémy 44
Bazin 84
Berthillon 24, 56
Betjamen & Barton 64
Bon 34
La Bonbonnière Saint-Honoré 64
La Bonbonnière de la Trinité 75
Boulangerie Beauvallet 34
Boutique Maille 64
Cacao et Chocolat 44
Calixte 24
Caviar Kaspia 64
Charcuterie Alsacienne 44
Charcuterie Charles 44
Charcuterie Coesnon 44
Chez Tachon 14
Christian Constant 46
Debauve & Gallais 14
Denise Acabo/À L'Étoile d'Or 75
Desgrippes 54
Drahonnet 24
Duchesne 54
Fauchon 65
La Ferme Saint Aubin 25
La Ferme St-Hubert 65
Florence Finkelsztajn 25
G Détou 15
Gérard Beaufort 34
Gosselin 15
Henri Ceccaldi 75
Izraël 25
Jean-Luc Poujauran 54
Jean-Paul Hévin 44, 46, 54
Jean-Pierre Carton 45
Julien 15, 65
Kayser 34
La Librairie des Gourmets 34
Librairie Gourmande 34
La Maison de la Truffe 65
La Maison du Chocolat 65
La Maison du Miel 75
Marcel Leverrier 15
Marie-Anne Cantin 55
Max Poilâne 15
Michel Brusa 35
Michel Chaudin 55
Olivier & Co 45
Le Pain au Naturel 84

Le Petit Bleu 85
Petrossian 55
Poilâne 45
René de Saint-Ouen 65
Ryst-Dupeyron 55
Sacha Finkelsztajn 25
Steff Le Boulanger 35
Stohrer 25
Verlet 15

MARKETS A–Z
Aligre markets 27, 85
Breteuil Market 55
Carmes Market 35
Marché Biologique 45
Popincourt Market 85
Richard-Lenoir Market 85
Rue de Buci Market 45
Rue Cler Market 55
Rue Montorgueil Market 15
Rue Mouffetard Market 35

PICNIC SITES A–Z
Parc du Champ de Mars 55

RESTAURANTS BY CUISINE

AMERICAN
Burger King 57
Chicago Meatpackers 57
Hard Rock Café 57, 66, 73
McDonald's 57
Planet Hollywood 66

ASIAN
Chez Vong 16

AUSTRALIAN
Woolloomooloo 17

CAMEROON
La Gazelle 17

CHINESE
Mirama 31
New Nioulaville 16
Le Président 16

FAMILY
Altitude 95 57, 76
Bistro Romain 56
Burger King 57
Chicago Meatpackers 57
Hard Rock Café 57, 66, 73

Hippo 56
Justine 57
McDonald's 57

FRENCH
L'Affriolé 48
Alcazar 39
Allard 39
À Sousceyrac 79
Au C'Amelot 79
Aux Charpentiers 39
Les Bacchantes 68
Le Balzar 28
La Bamboche 49
Le Bar au Sel 49
Benoit 19
Bofinger 19
Les Bouchons de François Clerc 87
Les Bookinistes 41
Le Bourdonnais 49
Le Buisson Ardent 28
La Casserole 17
Le Cave Drouot 68
Chez Henri au Moulin à Vent 28
Chez Jean 69
Chez Joël D – Bistro de l'Huître 29
Chez Michel 77, 79
Chez Paul 79
Chez René 29
Le Cinq 60
La Closerie des Lilas 41
Il Cortile 10
Le Coupe-Chou 29
Le Divellec 49
Écaille et Plume 51
Les Élyssées du Vernet 66
L'Épi Dupin 41
Les Fontaines 31
Le Grizzli 20
La Guirlande de Julie 20
Le Jardin 60
Les Jumeaux 80
Lapérouse 41, 66, 67
Maxim's 61
Le Moulin à Vins 70
Le Pactole 31
Paul Minchelli 51
Pharamond 66, 67
Le Poquelin 11
Le Relais Louis XIII 41
Le Restaurant de l'Astor 61
Restaurant Opéra 70
Restaurant du Palais-Royal 11
Le Roi du Pot au Feu 70

Spoon, Food and Wine 61
Taillevent 66
Le Train Bleu 77
La Verrière 71
Le Vieux Bistro 21
Le Villaret 81
Le Violon d'Ingres 51
La Zygotissoire 81

FRENCH HAUTE CUISINE
Alain Ducasse 58
Les Ambassadeurs 58
L'Ambroisie 19
L'Arpège 48
Le Carré des Feuillants 8
L'Espadon 10
Gérard Besson 10
Le Grand Véfour 11
Guy Savoy 60, 66
Jacques Cagna 41
Jules Verne 51, 76
Laurent 61
Pierre Gagnaire 61
La Tour d'Argent 31, 66

FRENCH REGIONAL
L'Alsaco 68
L'Ambassade d'Auvergne 19
La Bastide Odéon 40
Brasserie de L'Île St-Louis 20
Chez Catherine 69
Le Convivial 69
La Galoche d'Aurilliac 80
Pile ou Face 11

FRENCH TRADITIONAL
Au Pied de Cochon 8

FUSION
Jules Verne 51, 76

INDIAN
L'Étoile du Kashmir 79
La Ville de Jagannath 81

ITALIAN
Il Cortile 10
Gli Angeli 20

JAPANESE
Isse 11

JEWISH
Jo Goldenberg 21

SEAFOOD
Le Bar au Sel 49
Chez Joël D – Bistro de l'Huître 29
Le Divellec 49
Paul Minchelli 51

VEGETARIAN
La Ville de Jagannath 81

The Louvre and Les Halles

Les Halles was once described by writer Émile Zola as 'the belly of Paris', and though its famous market moved out to the suburbs many years ago, there are still cafés and bars that open all hours and keep up something of the old lively and raucous atmosphere. In contrast, the area around the Louvre and the nearby Palais-Royal has a grander air, with more elegant cafés and restaurants, but with plenty of more inexpensive places too, if you know where to look.

THE LOUVRE AND LES HALLES
Restaurants

Au Pied de Cochon ❶

6 r. Coquillaire
∅ 40 13 77 00
Ⓜ Les Halles métro
Open: daily 24 hours
Reservations unnecessary
All credit cards accepted
French traditional
€€

Onion soup and pigs' trotters are two long-standing favourites here, showing that hearty simple fare forms the core of the menu, though simple does not necessarily mean inexpensive. It's often packed and noisy, making for a terrific and buzzing atmosphere.

Le Carré des Feuillants ❷

14 r. de Castiglione
∅ 42 86 82 82
Ⓜ Tuileries métro
Open: Mon–Fri lunch and dinner, Sat dinner
Reservations essential
All credit cards accepted
French haute cuisine
€€€

A formal wood-panelled dining room but cuisine that reflects the chef's roots in the southwest: a delicious chestnut soup with white truffles is one seasonal starter, with eel ravioli or tasty scallops layered with celery and truffles among the other intriguing creations.

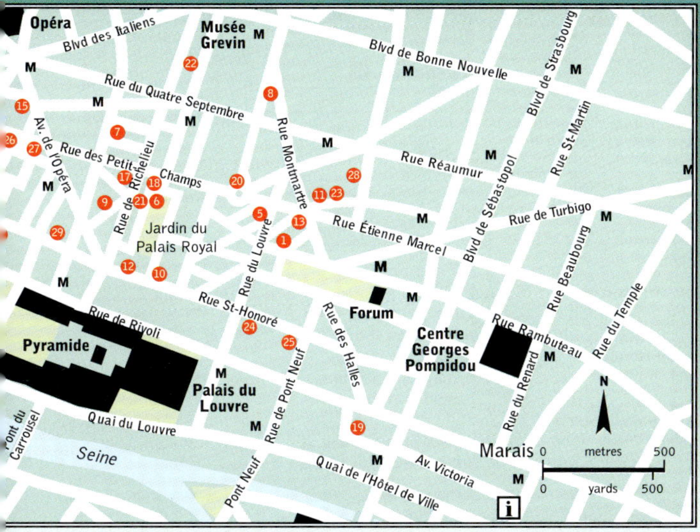
Opéra
Blvd des Italiens
Musée Grevin
Blvd de Bonne Nouvelle
Blvd de Strasbourg
Rue du Quatre Septembre
Rue Montmartre
Rue St-Martin
Av. de l'Opéra
Rue des Petit-Champs
Rue de Richelieu
Rue Réaumur
Blvd de Sébastopol
Rue de Turbigo
Rue Étienne Marcel
Jardin du Palais Royal
Rue du Louvre
Rue Beaubourg
Rue St-Honoré
Forum
Rue des Halles
Centre Georges Pompidou
Rue Rambuteau
Rue du Temple
Rue de Rivoli
Pyramide
Palais du Louvre
Rue de Pont Neuf
Rue du Renard
Quai du Louvre
Pont du Carrousel
Seine
Pont Neuf
Quai de l'Hôtel de Ville
Av. Victoria
Marais
metres
yards
N

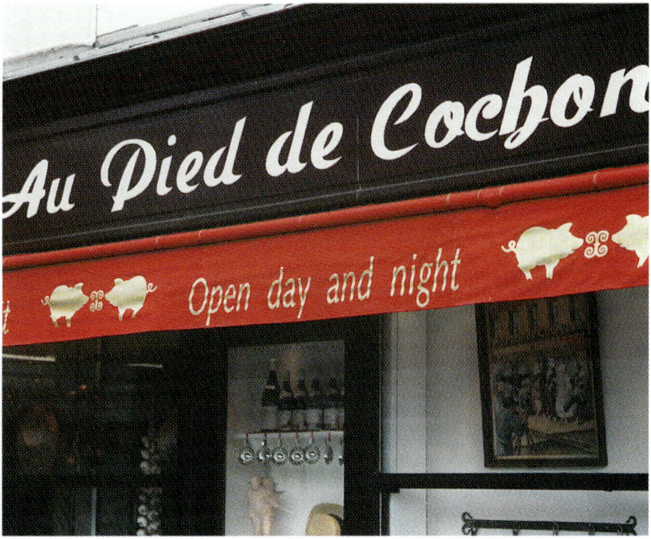
Au Pied de Cochon
Open day and night

Il Cortile ③

Hôtel Castille, 37 r. Cambon
∅ 44 58 45 67
Concorde or Madeleine métro
Open: Mon–Fri lunch and dinner
Reservations essential
All credit cards accepted
Italian-French
€€€

Ask for a courtyard table in summer, to sample the superb Italian food such as pasta in squid ink, prepared by a top French chef. Seafood is exceptionally good, as are favourite desserts such as *panna cotta* and tiramisu.

L'Espadon ④

Hôtel Ritz, 15 pl. Vendôme
∅ 43 16 30 80
Madeleine or Concorde métro
Open: daily lunch and dinner
Reservations recommended
All credit cards accepted
French haute cuisine
€€€

They don't come any ritzier than the Ritz, though the garden restaurant combines formal with informal and serves sumptuous dishes such as fillet of John Dory with olives and a saffron sauce. It also has one of the best dessert trolleys in Paris – a four-storey affair.

Gérard Besson ⑤

5 r. de Coq'Héron
∅ 42 33 14 74
Louvre métro
Open: Mon–Fri lunch and dinner, Sat dinner
Reservations essential
All credit cards accepted
French haute cuisine
€€€

Try the tasting menu in this highly-rated home of haute cuisine, which should include the chef's signature dessert:

▲ Il Cortile

candied fennel with vanilla ice cream, served with a sauce spiced with orange zest and coriander seeds.

Le Grand Véfour ⑥

17 r. de Beaujolais
⌀ 42 96 56 27
Ⓜ Palais-Royal métro
Open: Mon–Fri lunch and dinner; closed Aug
Reservations essential
All credit cards accepted
French haute cuisine
€€€

A 19th-century restaurant atmosphere but definitely modern creative cooking, with

lavish dishes such as ravioli stuffed with *foie gras* and served with a truffle sauce among the menu's highlights.

Isse ⑦

56 r. Ste-Anne
⌀ 42 96 67 76
Ⓜ Pyramides métro
Open: Tue–Fri lunch and dinner, Sat dinner; closed two weeks in Aug
Reservations recommended
Japanese
€€

You might not have considered eating Japanese in Paris, but this has some of the best sushi in the city, with the air of a typical French bistro. The sushi bar is downstairs and the slightly more formal eating upstairs. Try a giant sushi platter for two or more people.

Pile ou Face ⑧

52 bis r. Notre-Dame-des-Victoires
⌀ 42 33 64 33
Ⓜ Bourse métro
Open: Mon–Sat lunch and dinner
Reservations recommended
American Express
French regional
€€

This elegant restaurant with Normandy roots manages to be intimate and homely too, attracting customers from the nearby Bourse (Stock Exchange). Sample their trademark dish: rabbit seasoned with herbs, black peppercorns and cream and simmered for hours.

Le Poquelin ⑨

17 r. Molière
⌀ 42 96 22 19
Ⓜ Palais-Royal métro
Open: Mon–Fri lunch and dinner
Reservations essential
All credit cards accepted
French
€€

Kidneys with a Meaux mustard sauce is one of the classic dishes at this traditional restaurant which is cheerfully decorated in theatrical style. The *prix fixe* lunch menu is a good bargain, but prices are cheap given the standard of cooking.

Restaurant du Palais-Royal ⑩

110 galerie Valois
⌀ 40 20 00 27
Ⓜ Palais-Royal métro
Open: Mon–Sat lunch and dinner; closed Sat lunch in winter, also at Christmas and New Year
Reservations recommended
All credit cards accepted
French
€€

With great views over the Palais-Royal gardens, this is a good choice for summer days and nights. A bistro feel in historic surroundings with modern cooking of simple dishes such as steak tartare, grilled tuna or oysters.

The Louvre and Les Halles | 11

THE LOUVRE AND LES HALLES
Bars, cafés and pubs

Bar de l'Entr'acte

47 r. Montpensier

∅ 42 97 57 76

Palais-Royal métro

Open: daily from 1200, food lunch and dinner, Sun food 1200–1900

Reservations not allowed

Very lively bar-restaurant favoured by journalists and actors from the theatre across the road. Theatrical costumes are part of the décor, the food is safe but delicious, such as cheese tarts, and the wine is from the Loire Valley.

Le Café

62 r. Tiquetonne

∅ 40 39 08 00

Étienne-Marcel métro

Open: daily from 1000, food from 1200–2400

Reservations unnecessary

Fashionable hang-out on two floors, where the chic and the sleek sip their drinks and converse while eyeing the room. You don't come here to eat, although you can nibble a salad or another simple dish.

Café-Bar le Nemours

2 pl. Colette

∅ 42 61 34 14

Palais-Royal métro

Open: daily

Reservations unnecessary

Swish place by the Palais-Royal, where Parisian ladies with means sip coffee and look chic against the elegant backdrop. Simple snacks and salads are all that is on the menu, but it's the perfect place to pose.

Le Cochon à l'Oreille

15 r. Montmartre

∅ 42 36 07 56

Les Halles métro

Open: Mon–Sat 0700–1700, hot meals lunchtime only

Reservations unnecessary

No credit cards accepted

This ornate and muralled workingmen's café-bar harks back to the days of the market at Les Halles, and it still bustles in the early morning with the traders who linger in the region. A memorable atmosphere with cheap and cheerful food.

Colette

213 r. St-Honoré

∅ 55 35 33 90

Tuileries métro

Open: Mon–Sat 1030–1930, food 1130–1930

Reservations recommended

All credit cards accepted

Colette is a shop where style is everything, and they sell everything from food to electronic goods, as long as it looks cool. The downstairs café epitomises this, with dozens of types of bottled water, subtle snacks … and you can buy the

glassware and crockery if you like it.

Harry's Bar 15

5 r. Daunou

⌀ 42 61 71 14

Opéra métro

Open: Mon–Sat from 1030, food 1200–1500

Reservations not allowed

American Express

€€

There's a great atmosphere at this old favourite, where they claim to have invented the Bloody Mary in 1921 and to make the best dry martinis in Paris. The place is popular with tourists, locals and ex-pat Americans alike, making a lively mix.

Hemingway Bar 16

Hôtel Ritz, 15 pl. Vendôme

⌀ 43 16 30 30

Madeleine or Concorde métro

Open: Tue–Sat from 1830; closed July 25–Aug 25

Reservations not allowed

All credit cards accepted

€€€

Dine here among the ghosts of Hemingway and F. Scott Fitzgerald, but not at the prices they paid. Cocktails and other drinks are expensive, but you're paying for the Ritz style and ambience. Try the dry martini, favoured by Hemingway.

Juveniles 17

47 r. de Richelieu

⌀ 42 97 46 49

Palais-Royal métro

Open: Mon–Sat from 1200

Reservations recommended

€€

A sister to Willi's but much more emphatically geared to wine, with glasses and bottles from all round the world, and basic but tasty and filling food to soak up the alcohol, such as *tapas*, beef sandwiches and chicken salad.

Willi's Wine Bar 18

13 r. des Petits-Champs

⌀ 42 61 05 09

Pyramides métro

Open: Mon–Sat lunch and dinner

Reservations recommended

€€

A Paris wine bar run by two Englishmen sounds unlikely but Willi's is a raging success, serving up some of the best wine-bar food in the city. Main dishes change daily, but try their *chocolate au terrine* if it is on the dessert menu.

THE LOUVRE AND LES HALLES
Shops, markets and picnic sites

Shops

André Cleret [19]
4 r. des Lavandières-Ste-Opportune
∅ 42 33 82 68
◉ Châtelet métro
Open: Tue–Sat 0700–2000; closed part of July or Aug
No credit cards accepted

Cleret's is a bakery, but it's also much more than that, as they also provide incomparable sandwiches ... so you may well have to queue for such delights as ham and Gruyère cheese on a raisin and rye roll.

Au Panetier [20]
10 pl. des Petits-Pères
∅ 42 60 90 23
◉ Bourse métro
Open: Mon–Fri; closed July
No credit cards accepted

The late 19th-century interior is matched by the 1890s brick oven, which produces first-class baguettes: Parisians queue up even before the shop opens, as they only produce 250 of them – but there are other breads and rolls besides.

Chez Tachon [21]
38 r. de Richelieu
∅ 42 96 08 66
◉ Palais-Royal-Musée du Louvre métro
Open: Tue–Sat 0930–2000; closed lunchtimes and several weeks in July and Aug
No credit cards accepted

The kind of specialist shop that cheese-lovers dream of, with a knowledgeable owner who delights in the wide range and provides hand-written notes to describe each cheese, and also tell you which in his opinion are currently at their prime.

Debauve & Gallais [22]
33 r. Vivienne
∅ 40 39 05 50
◉ Bourse métro
Open: Mon–Sat 0900–1900; closed Sat in summer
VISA

A branch near the Bourse of the famous chocolatier in St-Germain, this dispenses the same wide array of sumptuous chocolates that will be impeccably wrapped and so make an ideal present – if you

can stop yourself from eating them first!

G Détou 23

58 r. Tiquetonne

⌀ 42 36 54 67

Ⓜ Les Halles or Étienne-Marcel métro

Open: Mon–Fri 0830–2100 and Sat am

No credit cards accepted

This general food store acts as a supplier of the very best ingredients to some of the city's leading chefs. From *foie gras* to dried apricots and catering-size bars of luxury chocolate, the shop is a treasure trove of up-market treats.

Gosselin 24

125 r. St-Honoré

⌀ 45 08 03 59

Ⓜ Louvre-Rivoli métro

Open: Tue–Sun 0700–2000; closed Aug

No credit cards accepted

The Parisian equivalent of a baker 'By Royal Appointment', as this shop supplies bread to the French President and others at the nearby Elysées Palace. The baker won the coveted 'Best Baguette' award in 1996.

Julien 25

75 r. St-Honoré

⌀ 42 36 24 83

Ⓜ Pont Neuf or Les Halles métro

Open: Mon–Sat 0630–2000

No credit cards accepted

Another simple but fashionable bakery in an area teeming with good-quality bread producers, this shop's baker, Jean-Noël Julien, has won first prize for the best baguette in Paris.

Marcel Leverrier 26

25 r. Danielle Casanova

⌀ 42 61 30 06

Ⓜ Pyramides métro

Open: Mon–Sat 0800–1345, Mon–Fri 1600–1915; closed Aug

Based in an art-deco building that is almost as worth seeing as the shop itself, this cheese shop offers an array of cheeses from all over France, including aged cheeses and young cheeses alike.

Max Poilâne 27

42 pl. du Marché St-Honoré

⌀ 42 61 10 53

Ⓜ Tuileries métro

Open: Mon–Sat 0830–1930

No credit cards accepted

Brother of the number one French bread-maker **Lionel** (*see page 45*), Max Poilâne also uses wood-fired ovens to produce his own version of the large country loaf, along with other delicious breads and rolls: the kind of shop where you want to bottle the smell.

Stohrer 28

51 r. Montorgueil

⌀ 42 33 38 20

Ⓜ Les Halles métro

Open: daily 0730–2030; closed two weeks in Aug

This famous patisserie has been in business since 1730, as it was right by the market at Les Halles, and has been a firm favourite since then. It sells great cakes, sweets and other treats, as well as bread.

Verlet 29

256 r. St-Honoré

⌀ 42 60 67 39

Ⓜ Palais-Royal-Musée du Louvre métro

Open: daily 0900–1900; closed weekends in summer and Sun and Mon in winter

This is the place to come if you want to find the best teas and coffees from all over the world, including Blue Mountain coffee from Jamaica and the best from the Arab world. A small café serves snacks, desserts and of course a range of fresh teas and coffees.

Markets

Rue Montorgueil Market 28

Ⓜ Les Halles métro

Open: Tue–Sat, and Sun am

This street market is one of the last links with Les Halles, the famous Parisian market that once existed here before being replaced with the modern shopping centre. Food and flower stalls fill the street, with plenty of sidewalk cafés so you can savour the atmosphere, if you find a seat.

Let them eat snake

Fancy a jellyfish salad?

French cuisine may dominate in Paris but it is still possible to eat in restaurants from almost every country in the world, with Italian, Indian and Chinese restaurants being especially popular. There are restaurants from the Congo and the Seychelles, from Russia and Romania, Switzerland and Senegal, Ethiopia, Cuba, Tibet, Venezuela, the Philippines, Korea, several from Brazil and even one from Britain.

Many diners might think French menus are exotic enough by themselves, featuring such delicacies as frogs' legs, snails, calves' heads, bone marrow, blackbird pâté, bull tartare, veal shin and the reproductive organs of various farm animals. But in among the many non-French menus are some even more unusual dishes that diners might wish to try ... or to avoid, according to taste.

Naturally, the city's Asian restaurants produce some dishes that even the French – not noted for squeamishness when it comes to eating any part of an animal – might think twice about tackling.

A dish that is not actually on the menu at **Chez Vong** (*10 r. de la Grand-Truanderie; ∅ 40 39 99 89; open: Mon–Sat lunch and dinner; reservations recommended; all credit cards accepted;* ❶❷❸) is stuffed snake fritters, but that is because the importation of reptiles is illegal, making it impossible to produce the dish on a regular basis. However, the chef will prepare the fritters, or a snake soup, if customers bring in their own – the opposite of a Chinese takeaway.

Le Président (*1st floor, r. du Faubourg-du-Temple 120–4; ∅ 47 00 17 18;* Ⓜ *Belleville métro; open: daily lunch and dinner; reservations unnecessary; all credit cards accepted;* ❶) is a huge and hugely popular Chinese restaurant, much favoured by wedding parties. This also has some intriguing items on the menu which reflect the difference in cultural, as well as gastronomic, tastes. The French and other nations may enjoy pigs' trotters, though far fewer are ready to try one of Le Président's renowned dishes: chicken feet. These are cubed and served in a salad with lemon and spices.

New Nioulaville (*r. de l'Orillon; ∅ 40 21 96 18;* Ⓜ *Belleville métro; open: daily lunch and dinner; reservations unnecessary;* 🗎 🗎 *American Express;* ❶) is yet another large Chinese place, which has seating

▲ Woolloomooloo

for 500 people and is noted for its eclectic menu that runs to 18 pages. Ox penis has featured here, but if you find that hard to swallow then perhaps their jellyfish salad might slip down a little easier, when sliced, fried and drizzled with peanut oil. Chinese wines and beers also feature here, although it has to be said that they make better beer than wine.

Woolloomooloo (*36 blvd Henri IV; ✆ 42 72 32 11; closed all day Mon and Tue lunch; reservations recommended;* 💳 🆅🅸🆂🅰 *American Express;* ❹❹) is that unusual thing, an Australian restaurant, and regularly has kangaroo on the menu, which is a very lean and healthy meat, and delicious if cooked properly, as it is here. It might be served as a starter, sliced in a salad, or as a main course, stir-fried: quick cooking is the secret with kangaroo, and no, it is not because you need to do it before it hops out of the pan. Woolloomooloo has also been known to serve ostrich meat, when it was in vogue.

Crocodile or alligator is a popular dish in many countries where it is plentiful, including the southern states of the USA. In Paris – where the Seine is crocodile-free – it is available at **La Gazelle** (*9 r. Rennequin, Paris 75017; ✆ 42 67 64 18; open: Mon–Sat lunch and dinner;* ❹❹). 'The Gazelle' is a Cameroon restaurant in the Monceaux district northwest of the city centre, and crocodile is served in a black sauce seasoned with seven spices, while smoked porcupine in a gumbo sauce has also been on the menu.

> **Crocodile is served in a black sauce seasoned with seven spices, while smoked porcupine in a gumbo sauce is also on the menu.**

Finally beaver, which is available at **La Casserole** (*17 r. Boinod, Paris 75018; ✆ 42 54 50 97; reservations recommended; all credit cards accepted;* ❹❹). The chef here is especially fond of game, and beaver is considered fair game and is served in a mushroom stew, tasting a little like rabbit or hare.

Let them eat snake | 17

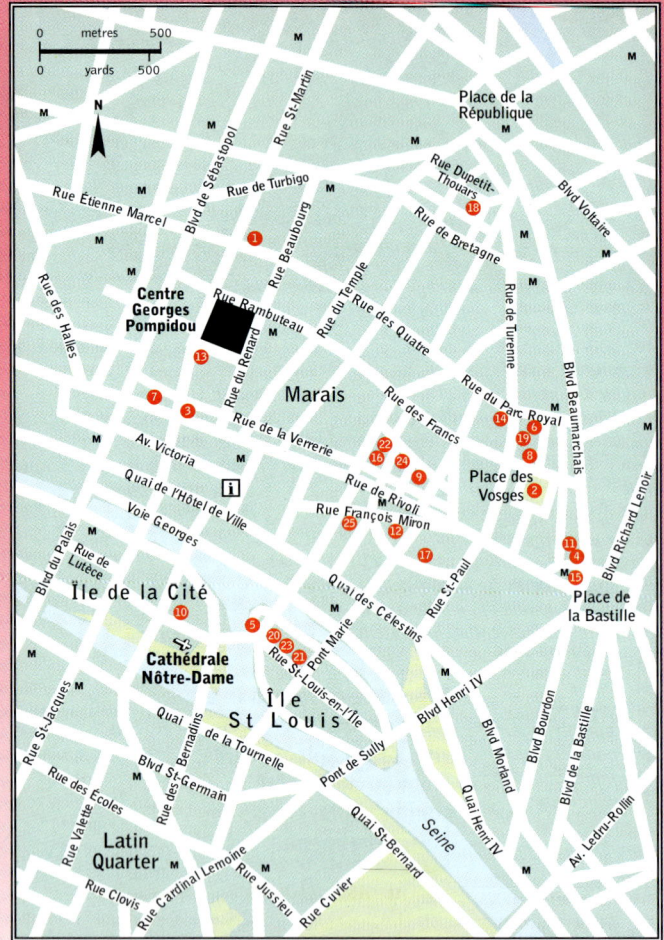

Temple, Marais and the Islands

The Marais district is well on the tourist map and this is reflected in the number of eating places there. The neighbouring Temple district is also benefiting from the numerous visitors to the Marais, while across the bridges on the islands in the Seine are some of the best restaurants and up-market food stores.

TEMPLE, MARAIS AND THE ISLANDS
Restaurants

L'Ambassade d'Auvergne

22 r. du Grenier-St-Lazare
∅ 42 72 31 22
Rambuteau métro
Open: daily lunch and dinner
Reservations recommended
American Express
French regional
€€

There are several excellent Auvergne restaurants in Paris and this is one of the best, with hearty dishes featuring pork and cabbage, and *aligot* (mashed potato, cheese and garlic), all in huge helpings, plus strong local cheeses and wines.

L'Ambroisie ❷

9 pl. des Vosges
∅ 42 78 51 45
Bastille or St-Paul métro
Open: Tue–Sat lunch and dinner; closed two weeks in spring and three weeks in Aug
Reservations essential
All credit cards accepted
French haute cuisine
€€€

One of Paris's temples of gastronomy, with formal décor and a reverential atmosphere, where you'll emerge with decidedly lighter pockets, but having had a meal to remember, filled with truffles, lobster, *foie gras* and other sumptuous luxuries.

Benoit

20 r. St-Martin
∅ 42 72 25 76
Hôtel-de-Ville métro
Open: daily lunch and dinner; closed Aug
Reservations recommended
American Express
French
€€€

Expensive for a bistro but the food merits it with superior versions of classic French dishes, such as chicken cooked in a salt crust and *blanquette* (veal in a cream sauce). Its dessert trolley is one of the best, too.

Bofinger

5–7 r. de la Bastille
∅ 42 72 87 82
Bastille métro

BRASSERIE
BOFINGER

Open: Mon–Fri lunch and dinner, Sat–Sun 1200–0100

Reservations recommended

All credit cards accepted

French

€€

In this Parisian institution in a wonderful art-nouveau building, good affordable food is as important as the surroundings. Options range from simple but tasty poached salmon to richer choices such as pan-fried duck *foie gras* with apples.

Brasserie de L'Île St-Louis

55 quai de Bourbon

⌀ 43 54 02 59

Ⓜ Pont-Marie métro

Open: Fri–Tue 1130–0100, Thu 1700–0100; closed Aug

Reservations recommended

€€

French regional

€€

Serving food from Alsace, this brasserie gives you the feeling that you have joined a private party in its small old-fashioned dining room. Sturdy country cooking dominates: try the *choucroute*, and one of the under-rated Alsatian wines.

Gli Angeli

5 r. St-Gilles

⌀ 42 71 05 80

Ⓜ Chemin Vert métro

Open: daily lunch and dinner; closed two weeks in Aug

Reservations recommended

€€

Italian

€€

Handy for the place des Vosges, this southern Italian restaurant serves simple but delicious pasta and other dishes, including a fabulous tiramisu, with great attention to fresh ingredients and a typically Italian friendly service.

Le Grizzli

7 r. St-Martin

⌀ 48 87 77 56

Ⓜ Hôtel-de-Ville or Châtelet métro

Open: Mon–Sat lunch and dinner

Reservations recommended

€€ American Express

French

€€

Although décor is unpretentious, a superior bistro menu sets this place apart from the rest. Try the house speciality, *fricot de veau*, a stew of veal shoulder cooked in wine, herbs, mushrooms and other vegetables.

La Guirlande de Julie

25 pl. des Vosges

⌀ 48 87 94 07

Ⓜ Bastille or St-Paul métro

Open: Wed–Sun lunch and dinner

Reservations recommended

All credit cards accepted

20 | Temple, Marais and the Islands

French

€€

From the man who owns the legendary **Tour d'Argent** (*see pages 31 and 66*), Claude Terrail, this less formal place with some outside tables also offers exquisite cuisine, including a classic *pot-au-feu* and a superb crème brûlée.

Jo Goldenberg

7 r. des Rosiers
✆ 48 87 20 16
Ⓜ St-Paul métro
Open: daily 1200–2400
Reservations recommended
All credit cards accepted
Jewish

€€

The most famous Jewish restaurant in Paris, though recommended more for atmosphere and history than for the cooking. Stick to the staples such as chicken soup with *matzoh* balls or *borscht*, or the *zakouski*, and you won't go far wrong.

Le Vieux Bistro

14 r. de Cloître-Nôtre-Dame
✆ 43 54 18 95
Ⓜ St-Michel-Nôtre-Dame RER or Cité métro
Open: daily lunch and dinner
Reservations recommended

French

€€

Right alongside Nôtre-Dame, this traditional bistro with wooden tables and candles in bottles is filled with Parisians who appreciate its excellent preparation of old favourites, such as boeuf bourguignon or lemon tart.

TEMPLE, MARAIS AND THE ISLANDS
Bars, cafés and pubs

L'Aréa ⑪

10 r. des Tournelles
⌀ 42 72 96 50
Bastille métro
Open: Tue–Sun dinner; closed two weeks in Aug
Reservations unnecessary
💳 VISA
Brazilian-Lebanese
€€

Brash and fashionable mix of bar and restaurant with live music on some nights, this will appeal to younger travellers who want to see where Parisians regard as chic. Try the Brazilian black bean and pork stew, or just relax with a beer or excellent Lebanese wine.

The Auld Alliance ⑫

80 r. François Miron
⌀ 48 04 30 40
St-Paul métro
Open: daily from 1100, food Mon–Fri lunch and dinner, Sat lunch and Sun 1200–1900
Reservations not allowed
💳 VISA
French-Scottish
€€

This Scottish pub has a friendly atmosphere and makes a welcome change from French bars, if you want to sample Scottish beers on draught or in bottles, or its range of whiskies. Most people go to drink rather than to eat, and the bar food fills a gap rather than being a gourmet experience.

Café Beaubourg ⑬

43 r. St-Merri
⌀ 48 87 63 96
Châtelet-Les-Halles RER or Hôtel-de-Ville métro
Open: daily
Reservations unnecessary
All credit cards accepted
French
€

▲ The Auld Alliance

Overlooking the newly revamped Centre Pompidou, this place also draws attention to its own design, a mix of ancient and cool modern. Food is simple but tasty enough, with a flash-fried steak tartare being one of the recommendations.

Café des Musées ⑭

49 r. de Turenne
⌀ 42 72 96 17
Chemin Vert or St-Paul métro
Open: daily all day, hot meals from 1200
Reservations unnecessary
No credit cards accepted
French
€€

Named after the Picasso and other museums nearby, at mealtimes this is as much restaurant as café, serving dishes such as coq au vin, although snacks are available all day. It's worth seeking out if you are in the Marais.

Café des Phares 15

7 pl. de la Bastille	
⌀ 42 72 04 70	
Bastille métro	
Open: daily	
Reservations unnecessary	
No credit cards accepted	
French	
€	

Right on the busy place de la Bastille, this is great for people- (and traffic-) watching, with more stimulating options on a Sunday morning when philosophy discussions are held. You might prefer simply to muse on the relative merits of a beer or a glass of wine.

Café du Trésor 16

5 r. du Trésor	
⌀ 44 78 06 60	
Hôtel-de-Ville or St-Paul métro	
Open: daily	
Reservations unnecessary	

French	
€€	

Very fashionable café in the Marais with a DJ each night playing the latest and loudest sounds to a crowd so hip it hurts. The outside tables are more relaxing at the end of a traffic-free cul-de-sac.

Chez Karine 17

16 r. Charlemagne

⌀ 42 72 14 16
St-Paul métro
Open: Mon–Sat, food served lunch and dinner
Reservations unnecessary
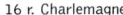
French-Polish
€

This mix of café, shop, bar and restaurant looks very unprepossessing from the outside but inside has a characterful mix of people and a friendly atmosphere. The food is simple stuff but the Polish take on French fare is unusual and good.

Web Bar 18

32 r. de Picardie
⌀ 42 72 66 55
République métro
Open: daily, food from 1130–2330
Reservations unnecessary

French
€

Much more than the cyber café the name indicates, this is an often raucous bar serving good drinks, OK food and also dishing up regular events, everything from poetry nights to party and dance nights.

TEMPLE, MARAIS AND THE ISLANDS
Shops, markets and picnic sites

Shops

Au Levain du Marais

32 r. de Turenne
⌀ 42 78 07 31
St-Paul métro
Open: Mon–Sat 0700–2000
No credit cards accepted

This excellent Marais bakery, housed in a 100-year-old building, offers both traditional and new breads with unusual flavours such as a raisin rye bread. Wonderful cakes, pastries and tarts too.

Berthillon

31 r. St-Louis-en-l'Île
⌀ 43 54 31 61
Pont-Marie métro
Open: Wed–Sun 1000–2000; closed Easter and July/Aug
No credit cards accepted

The best ice cream in Paris is what local people claim, and to prove it they're prepared to queue alongside curious and knowledgeable tourists to take their pick from over 60 flavours on offer, along with sorbets and *granités*.

Calixte

64 r. St-Louis-en-l'Île
⌀ 43 26 42 28
Pont-Marie métro
Open: Fri–Wed 0930–1930 (1830 on Sun); closed lunchtime and Aug
No credit cards accepted

This little gem is hidden away on the Île St-Louis, and if you are self-catering you could stock up for days on its range of treats, from starters through to desserts. It makes perfect croissants every morning, pâtés and terrines, and desserts you normally only see on trolleys at the best restaurants.

Drahonnet

32 r. Vieille-du-Temple
⌀ 42 72 78 01
St-Paul métro
Open: Fri–Wed 0700–2130 (from 0800 Sun); closed Aug
No credit cards accepted

If you're looking for picnic ingredients in the

▲ Au Levain du Marais

Marais, check out this fabulous bakery which makes all kinds of delicious croissants, rolls, baguettes and loaves, including rye and walnut breads.

La Ferme Saint Aubin ㉓

76 r. St-Louis-en-l'Île

∅ 43 54 74 54

◉ Pont-Marie or Sully-Morland métro

Open: Tue–Sun 0800–2000 (closes 1300–1500 Sun only)

No credit cards accepted

Even if you don't like cheese, the visual and sensory appeal of shops like this can't be beaten, with its rows of small round cheeses and displays of larger ones from all over France, from Normandy through to the Pyrenees.

Florence Finkelsztajn ㉔

24 r. des Écouffes

∅ 48 87 92 85

◉ St-Paul métro

Open: Thu–Mon 1000–1900; closed lunchtime and Aug

No credit cards accepted

One of the two Finkelsztajn pastry shops in Paris's Jewish quarter, with Jewish rye bread freshly baked, and a delicatessen where you could put together a great picnic with smoked fish and a range of dips to go with the bread and cakes.

Izraël ㉕

30 r. François Miron

∅ 42 72 66 23

◉ Hôtel-de-Ville métro

Open: Tue–Sat from 0930; closed Aug

This wonderful Aladdin's cave of a shop stocks the best produce from around the world, ranging from rum from Guadeloupe or Russian vodka to English mustard and Greek feta cheese. Great for making picnics or tracking down unusual herbs and spices.

Sacha Finkelsztajn ㉒

27 r. des Rosiers

∅ 42 72 78 91

◉ St-Paul métro

Open: Wed–Sun 1000–1900; closed lunchtime and July

No credit cards accepted

The second Finkelsztajn shop is similar to the first; this is the place to try the family's freshly made cheesecake (ask for *vatrouchka*) which is made every afternoon. Many other fresh cakes and pastries too.

Promenades Gourmandes

Discover food heaven

Paule Caillat tells me as we snoop around the **Popincourt market** (*see page 85*) 'Here's a stall that's a dying breed'. 'It's a *triperie*, which sells offal. This *rognon de veau* or veal kidney is the finest quality, take a look. These veal tongues are delicious. That plate there of *onglets*, that's a delicious cut of meat from the spine and is also known as *le morçeau de boucher*, the butcher's piece, because it was so good that the butchers used to steal it for themselves.'

Paule is Paris born and bred and gives tourists a taster of Parisian cuisine by leading her **Promenades Gourmandes** (Ø *48 04 56 84*) around the city. Every tour is different, as Paule will first call you to discuss what your interests are. I tell her I am interested in seeing good food markets, some specialist food shops and in getting her tips for the best places to eat.

The Popincourt market is five minutes from my hotel, and soon we are checking out its stalls, *triperie* and all. 'The market is always much quieter on a Tuesday; you should come back on Friday when it is generally busier.'

We walk between the rows of stalls and I marvel at both the quality and quantity of food on display. I sniff the earthy smell of the mushroom stalls, passing on to the salty tang from the buckets of shellfish. The rows of cheeses look wonderfully tempting, runny bries demanding to be eaten, perhaps with an oven-fresh loaf from the bread stall next door.

'If you're buying something to take back home,' Paule advises, 'look for the *Producteur* sign above a stall. It means they grow their own produce, mostly. Some will sell other things ... this guy here has obviously not grown those lemons in the middle of winter, but most of the stuff here is his own. And this stall here, the owner has his own orchards about 50km north of Paris, and he comes to this market every week to sell his apples and his cider. This stall is from Le Savoie, all produce from the Alps. For me as a cook the product is the beginning of everything. You can have the finest of recipes but if the ingredients aren't top quality then forget it.'

We hop on the métro and Paule takes me next to the **Aligre markets** (*see page 85*) off Faubourg St-Antoine, east of the Bastille. She tells me it's the most colourful market in Paris, and I can quite believe it. In the permanent covered market there is the top produce. 'But of course very expensive,' says Paule. I see fresh truffles, rows of pheasants waiting to be taken home and plucked, even a whole wild boar suspended from one meat stall. 'And look at the price of *colinot*,' Paule says. 'It's 99F a kilo, back at Popincourt one fish stall was selling it for 35F!'

Outside there are the cheaper food stalls, mostly run by Moroccans, Algerians and Tunisians. 'They're terrific at bargaining,' Paule tells me, 'so they get the best prices from the wholesalers and sell very cheaply here, but you have to watch what you're buying as they mix the poor stuff up with the good.' The third market at Aligre is a junk market, what the Americans would call 'a Five and Dime': second-hand goods.

We walk around Bastille to the **rue St-Antoine**, which Paule recommends if you want to see specialist food shops. There are cheese shops and patisseries, and even a horsemeat shop. 'These are disappearing too,' Paule says, admitting that she has never tried horsemeat herself. 'It is supposed to be a very healthy meat. It's very cheap, but we don't kill horses specially to eat them. No, it's meat from horses that have died naturally, a cheap source of meat for poor people in the past.'

Paule then takes me to one of the most wonderful little food shops I've ever been in, **Izraël's Le Monde des Épices** (*see page 25*). A million smells assault the senses, and show that the French don't only eat French produce. There are Turkish lentils, feta cheese from Greece, rum from Guadeloupe, vanilla pods from Tahiti, black peppercorns from Sarawak, Polish honey liqueur ... the list is endless.

> I sniff the earthy smell of the mushroom stalls, passing on to the salty tang from the buckets of shellfish.

We waltz through the Marais, Paule blending her food advice with historical anecdotes and personal history: this is the district in which she grew up, though her walks can take place in any district you want to explore. She is familiar with them all – a woman who certainly knows her onions!

The Latin Quarter

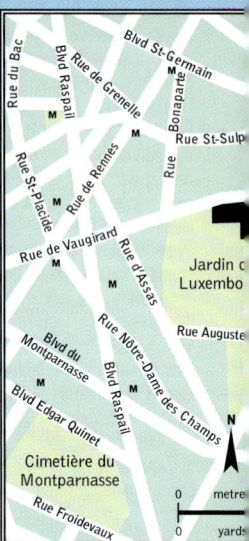

The bohemian Latin Quarter has always been known for its jazz clubs and student cafés, and food lovers will find it gives one of the widest variety of choices in the city, from top-class restaurants such as La Tour d'Argent to many cheap and cheerful ethnic eating places that reflect its multi-cultural nature.

THE LATIN QUARTER
Restaurants

Le Balzar ❶
49 r. des Écoles
⌀ 43 54 13 67
Ⓜ Cluny La Sorbonne métro
Open: daily from 1200
Reservations recommended
💳 American Express
French
€€

A venerable brasserie which continues to serve French classics much as it has done for decades. Expect few surprises, but if you want to sample the perfect onion soup or sole meunière, then this is the place to come.

Le Buisson Ardent ❷
25 r. Jussieu
⌀ 43 54 93 02
Ⓜ Jussieu métro
Open: Mon–Fri lunch and dinner, Sat dinner; closed Aug and Christmas
Reservations recommended
💳 American Express
French
€€

A comparatively new bistro that looks set to join the many venerable favourites in this district. The bright décor suits the light touches with the food, and main courses such as pork on a bed of lentils with *foie gras* will satisfy the heartiest appetite.

Chez Henri au Moulin à Vent ❸
20 r. des Fossés-St-Bernard
⌀ 43 54 99 37
Ⓜ Jussieu métro
Open: Tue–Sat lunch and dinner; closed Aug
Reservations recommended

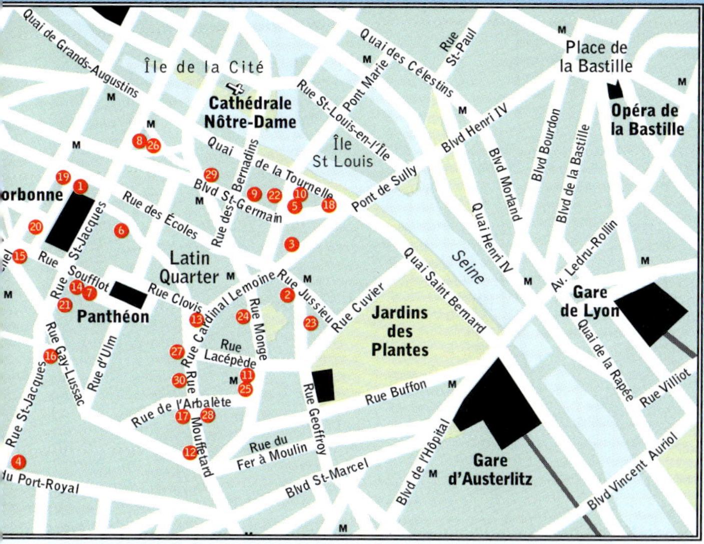

French

Long-established Parisian bistro which makes no concession to fashions in décor or cuisine. Superb traditional dishes such as *foie gras*, *escargots*, steaks and rich delicious puddings abound – not for those with light appetites.

Chez Joël D – Bistro de l'Huître

285 r. St-Jacques
43 54 71 70
Port Royal RER
Open: Tue–Sat lunch and dinner
Reservations recommended

French-Seafood

A fair walk from the heart of the Latin Quarter, but that means fewer tourists. It's also a walk worth making for lovers of oysters and other shellfish and seafood: the name means the Oyster Bistro, so what else would you want to eat?

Chez René

14 blvd St-Germain
43 54 30 23
Maubert-Mutualité métro
Open: Mon–Fri lunch and dinner, Sat dinner; closed Aug
Reservations recommended

French

In an area not short of eating places, Chez René has survived for over forty years, by serving up reliable fare that appeals as much to local people as to the many tourists who flock here. Try coq au vin, followed by a delicious tart for dessert.

Le Coupe-Chou

11 r. de Lanneau
46 33 68 69
Maubert-Mutualité métro
Open: Mon–Sat lunch and dinner, Sun dinner
Reservations recommended
American Express

French

The Latin Quarter | 29

Characterful and always busy place in a one-time barbershop, with good fixed-price menus and exemplary versions of such classic dishes as boeuf bourguignon, steak tartare or a creamy crème brûlée.

Les Fontaines ❼

9 r. Soufflot
∅ 43 26 42 80
Ⓜ Luxembourg RER
Open: Mon–Sat lunch and dinner
Reservations recommended
💳 VISA
French
€€

An unpretentious bistro that looks no different from hundreds of others in Paris, yet serves up excellent food in generous portions. Lovers of game will appreciate the robust dishes, such as wild boar, but try the chicory and blue cheese salad too.

Mirama ❽

17 r. St-Jacques
∅ 43 54 71 11
Ⓜ St-Michel métro
Open: daily from 1200
Reservations recommended
💳 VISA
Chinese
€

It may seem perverse to go to Paris and eat Chinese food, but this simple and busy place has a huge menu that may include dishes you never see back home.

Peking duck with honey is one terrific combination.

Le Pactole ❾

44 blvd St-Germain
∅ 46 33 31 31
Ⓜ Maubert-Mutualité métro
Open: Mon–Fri lunch and dinner, Sat dinner
Reservations recommended
💳 VISA American Express
French
€€

Tartare flambéed with cognac is one exciting dish from this fairly new restaurant with clean and bright lines that has become a fashionable favourite. Mediterranean scorpion fish with a bacon cream sauce is another daring combination.

La Tour d'Argent ❿

15–17 quai de la Tournelle
∅ 43 54 23 31
Ⓜ Maubert-Mutualité métro
Open: Tue–Sun lunch and dinner
Reservations essential
All credit cards accepted
French haute cuisine
€€€

One of the best restaurants in the city, and it certainly has some of the finest views. Ask for a table overlooking Nôtre-Dame, and settle in for a feast, of which peaches flambéed in raspberry liqueur give a flavour of the tempting desserts.

THE LATIN QUARTER
Bars, cafés and pubs

Café de la Poste

7 r. de l'Épée-de-Bois

☏ 43 37 05 58

Ⓜ Place Monge métro

Open: daily from 0815, hot meals lunch and dinner; closed three weeks in Aug

Reservations not allowed

No credit cards accepted

€

This may sound like a café for postal workers, which indeed it is, but this being Paris it's rather more sophisticated than that implies, with cool jazz and blues music, and satisfying simple meals that appeal to budget diners.

Les Caves de Bourgogne

144 r. Mouffetard

☏ 47 07 82 80

Ⓜ Censier-Daubentin métro

Open: Tue–Sun, hot meals Tue–Sat lunch and dinner, Sun snacks all day

Reservations unnecessary

€

This is a surprisingly fashionable bar in the street known for simplicity. It does a bargain three-course lunch (Tue–Sat) but otherwise it's a place to hang out, have a drink and a sandwich, while watching the market through the huge windows.

La Chope Café

2–4 pl. de la Contrescarpe

☏ 43 26 51 26

Ⓜ Place Monge or Cardinal Lemoine métro

Open: daily from 0800, food from 1200

Reservations not allowed

€

This great little bar has seating on an old Latin Quarter square, which hasn't changed too much since Ernest Hemingway lived round the corner. It's a place to chill out with a wine or beer, a snack or a salad.

Flowers Café

5 r. Soufflot

☏ 43 54 75 36

Ⓜ Luxembourg RER or Cluny La Sorbonne métro

Open: daily from 0600

Reservations unnecessary

€

With a view of the Panthéon and not far from the Sorbonne, this is a destination for students and tourists alike, whether in the inside casual restaurant or outside on the terrace with a drink or a basic café snack.

La Gueuze

19 r. Soufflot
✆ 43 54 63 00
Ⓜ Luxembourg RER or Cluny La Sorbonne métro
Open: daily from 1200
Reservations unnecessary
💳 💳 American Express
€

Beer lovers should make a pilgrimage to this bar which has one of the best-stocked beer lists in Paris, with usually a dozen or so available on draught and another 100 to 150 by the bottle. The beers are from all over the world but mainly Belgium. Food takes second place but is still decent fare.

Le Mauzac

7 r. de l'Abbé de l'Epée
✆ 46 33 75 22
Ⓜ Luxembourg or Port Royal RER
Open: Mon–Fri 0730–2230, Sat 0730–1600, food daily at lunch, dinner Thu and Fri (by reservation only); closed Easter, Christmas and three weeks in Aug
Reservations essential Thu and Fri dinner only otherwise reservations unnecessary
💳 💳
€€

This wine bar near the Luxembourg Gardens is off the tourist track so gives a good flavour of the real Paris and is a fantastic place for relaxing. Food tends towards steaks and other meat dishes, with salads, soups and of course a broad selection of wines.

Le Mouffetard

116 r. Mouffetard
✆ 43 31 42 50
Ⓜ Censier-Daubenton métro
Open: Tue–Sun from 0730; closed July
Reservations not allowed
American Express
€

A focus for the daily market in the same street, the café serves up breakfasts, lunches, dinners, snacks or just drinks from early morning till early evening. Don't expect haute cuisine, just decent affordable food, but it's definitely high on market atmosphere.

Le Rallye

11 quai de la Tournelle
✆ 43 54 29 65
Ⓜ Jussieu métro
Open: daily, hot meals only at lunch
Reservations unnecessary
No credit cards accepted
€

This is as basic a place as you'll get, right by the Seine, with a jukebox and a pinball machine, lots of locals who all know each other, and a place for tourists who want a touch of ordinary life in the city centre.

Le Reflet

6 r. Champollian
✆ 43 29 97 27
Ⓜ Cluny La Sorbonne métro
Open: daily from 1000, food from 1200
Reservations unnecessary
💳 💳
€

This is the kind of intellectual hangout that you hope to find in the Latin Quarter, with students and media professionals talking loudly about the arts and politics, drinking wine or coffee and snacking on simple food.

Tabac de la Sorbonne

7 pl. de la Sorbonne
✆ 43 54 52 04
Ⓜ St-Michel métro
Open: daily
Reservations unnecessary
No credit cards accepted
€

With a name like this you can expect it to be filled with smoke and students, and it is, and with others still living the bohemian life. Food consists of basic steaks, salads and sandwiches, but the atmosphere is good … if smoky.

THE LATIN QUARTER
Shops, markets and picnic sites

Shops

Bon

159 r. St-Jacques
⌀ 43 54 26 44
Luxembourg RER
Open: Tue–Sat 0730–2000; closed Sun pm and Aug
American Express

One of the area's delicious patisseries, and apart from chocolate, strawberry, lemon and other fruit tarts, a speciality is a fat-free lemon cheesecake called *gâteau fromage blanc 0%*.

Boulangerie Beauvallet

6 r. de Poissy
⌀ 43 26 94 24
Maubert-Mutualité métro
Open: Thu–Tue 0715–2000; closed part of July or Aug
No credit cards accepted

The sign of a good bakery is how quickly it sells out, which means you should get there early for the fresh baguettes and rolls, which the shop also supplies to several of the Latin Quarter restaurants.

Gérard Beaufort

6 r. Linné
⌀ 47 07 10 94
Jussieu métro
Open: Mon–Fri 0730–2000; closed Aug
American Express

From a croissant for breakfast to a strawberry tart to finish off a meal, this patisserie has a range of top-quality foods, as well as a small café in which to sample some of them.

Kayser

8 r. Monge
⌀ 44 07 01 42
Maubert-Mutualité métro
Open: Wed–Mon 0700–2000
No credit cards accepted

The owner of this shop near the rue Mouffetard market (*see page 35*), Eric Kayser, is a gifted baker as you will know as soon as you bite into one of his loaves, baguettes or tarts, or one of the sandwiches such as goats' cheese with pear.

La Librairie des Gourmets

98 r. Monge
⌀ 43 31 16 42
Censier-Daubenton métro
Open: Mon–Sat 1030–1900; closed Mon in Aug
American Express

Handy for the **rue Mouffetard market** (*see page 35*), this bright bookstore has over 2 500 titles on food and wine, with naturally the vast majority in French but there are some in other languages, including English. It's a good place to learn what food and wine events are on in the city too.

Librairie Gourmande

4 r. Dante
⌀ 43 54 37 27
Maubert-Mutualité métro
Open: daily 1000–1900

Just off the boulevard St-Germain is this magnet for lovers of the cookbook, recognisable

▲ Librairie Gourmande

▲ Michel Brusa

by its table of bargain books outside, mostly in French. In addition to the shelves of books inside, you can also buy attractive postcards and posters, which would look good in the kitchen.

Michel Brusa 27

16 r. Mouffetard

✆ 47 07 06 36

Place Monge or Cardinal Lemoine métro

Open: Mon–Sat 0730–2100; closed part of July or Aug

No credit cards accepted

If you've stocked up on picnic fare at the rue Mouffetard market (*see below*), then here's one place to add some bread or rolls, their sourdough baguettes coming highly recommended.

Steff Le Boulanger 28

123 r. Mouffetard

✆ 47 07 35 96

Censier-Daubenton métro

Open: Tue–Sun 0700–2000 (to 1400 Sun)

No credit cards accepted

Bang in the middle of the rue Mouffetard market, you won't find better breads with which to eat your cheeses, meats, olives and other goodies than these from Stephane Delauney. Try the wheat bread he's noted for, the *flûte Gana*.

Markets

Carmes market 29

Pl. Maubert

Maubert-Mutualité métro

Open: Tue, Thu and Sat

Only a small market by Parisian standards with less than 50 stalls, but it makes up for the size with the bustle on a Saturday morning when people come to buy the organic and specialist produce: mushrooms, olives, olive oil, herbs and the usual fruit and vegetables too.

Rue Mouffetard market 30

Place Monge or Censier-Daubenton métro

Open: Tue–Sat all day and Sun am

One of the best-known street markets in Paris in this former cheap bohemian district which is now also on the visitors' map. Food stalls are crammed into the narrow street, which is lined by excellent specialist food shops and cafés, and at weekends somehow a few buskers squeeze themselves into the crowds as well. There's a wide choice of eating places too, especially in the quieter side streets.

▲ Rue Mouffetard Market

Street food

The naming game

Paris has no great tradition of street food, such as you find in the Far East or even in some other European countries such as Holland and Belgium. But then why should the French snack in the streets when bistros, bakers, delicatessens, patisseries and chocolate shops seem to exist on almost every corner? One snacking tradition the Parisians do have is when buying a baguette, which you will frequently see tucked under someone's arm as they walk home with it. What you will see just as frequently if you look closely is that the end will have been broken off, as the tradition is to eat the end before you arrive home.

However, Paris does have a vast number of streets whose very names indicate the enthusiasm – obsession even – which the city has always had with food and drink. Take a look at those distinctive blue street signs as you explore the city, some of which will be familiar and some less so, but many of them will tell you something of the city's gastronomic history.

Let's start with the staples of bread and water. **Rue des Boulangers** in the Latin Quarter acquired its name in 1844 when it was indeed the 'Street of the Bakers', although not a single one remains today. **Rue Brisemiche** near the Centre Pompidou translates as 'Break-Bread Street', as it was here in the Middle Ages that clergy used to dispense free bread to the poor. The 'Street of the Millers' is **rue des Meuniers**, to the southeast in the 12th *arrondissement* where there was a flourmill back in the 18th century.

Rue des Eaux (in the 16th *arrondissement*) is the 'Street of the Waters', as it was here, in 1650 when the road was built, that workmen discovered a source of mineral water. Water was taken from here right through till the 18th century when the source dried up, but the name remains to this day.

For the wine on this list there is **rue des Morillons** in the 15th

arrondissement. The Morillon is a grape variety once grown in this district, producing some of the wine that Paris was noted for, and still produces today (*see pages 86–7*).

Fish features strongly on the menu of Paris street names, with a **rue des Poissonniers** in the 18th district behind the Gare du Nord and a boulevard Poissonière which runs between the 2nd and the 9th districts and which has a rue Poissonnière joining it. The boulevard goes back to 1685 when it was on the route the fish merchants from Calais took as they made their way to the great Paris market at Les Halles. The Marais has an Impasse de la Poissonnèrie, simply named as there was a fishmonger next to it.

From fish to meat, and meat of a very French kind, which was once sold in the **Impasse du Marché aux Cheveaux**, or 'Street of the Horse Market', a tiny stretch of road south of the Jardin des Plantes in the 5th district. **Rue de la Faisanderie** in the 16th *arrondissement* is named after the pheasant reserve that existed here in the more rural past.

> **Rue Brisemiche translates as 'Break-Bread Street', as it was here in the Middle Ages that clergy used to dispense free bread to the poor.**

The vegetarian option is **rue des Maraîchers** way out in the 20th *arrondissement*, which is where there were many market gardens (*maraîchers*) in the 18th century. In the 17th *arrondissement* there were also lots of farms, till as recently as the start of the 19th century, and hence **rue des Fermiers**, or 'Street of the Farmers'.

For the final course on the menu, **passage de la Brie** out in the 19th district needs no translating, taking its name from the region to the east of the city where the famous soft cheese is made.

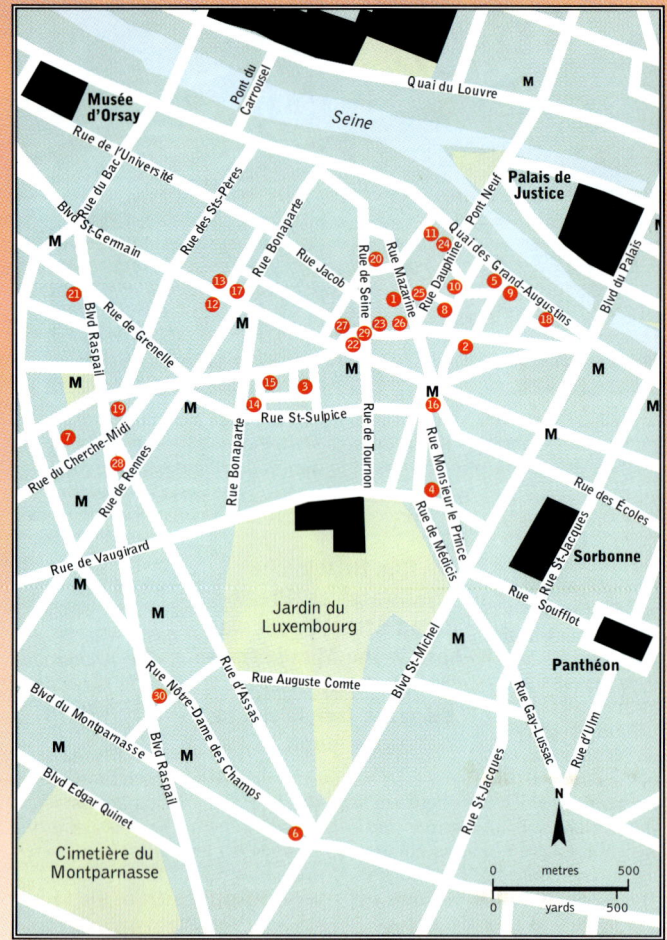

St-Germain

St-Germain is the haunt of writers and artists, with the likes of Hemingway and Sartre eating and drinking here, most notably in famous cafés such as Café de Flore and Les Deux Magots. Today they may attract as many tourists as locals, but the atmosphere still lingers. The area also has one of Paris's best street markets, in the rue de Buci.

ST-GERMAIN
Restaurants

Alcazar ❶

62 r. Mazarine	
✆ 53 10 19 99	
Odéon métro	
Open: daily lunch and dinner	
Reservations recommended	
All credit cards accepted	
French	
€€	

British designer and restaurateur Sir Terence Conran had the audacity to open a restaurant in Paris serving French food, and Alcazar is stylishly designed, as is the food, though you could eat fish and chips at the bar just to sample the style.

Allard

41 r. St-André-des-Arts	
✆ 43 26 48 23	
Odéon métro	
Open: Mon–Sat lunch and dinner; closed three weeks in Aug	
Reservations recommended	
All credit cards accepted	
French	
€€	

Long-established classic restaurant serving traditional dishes in an exemplary manner, with Burgundy snails a regular feature. Desserts such as the *symphonie aux trois chocolats* should satisfy the most demanding appetite.

Aux Charpentiers ❸

10 r. Mabillon	
✆ 43 26 30 05	
Mabillon métro	
Open: daily lunch and dinner	
Reservations recommended	

All credit cards accepted

French

❷ ❸

Named after the local Carpenters' Guild, here you dine, surrounded by local woodworkers' craft, on traditional bistro dishes such as grilled lamb chops flavoured with rosemary. *Blanquette* (veal in cream) is a speciality.

La Bastide Odéon ❹

7 r. Corneille

✆ 43 26 03 65

🚇 Odéon métro or Luxembourg RER

Open: Tue–Sat lunch and dinner; closed three weeks in Aug

Reservations recommended

💳 American Express

French regional

❷ ❸

▲ St-Germain-des-Prés

This smart Provençal bistro serves creative dishes made from the finest ingredients from southern France, such as rabbit stuffed with aubergine and age-old staples like sheeps' feet.

Les Bookinistes

53 quai des Grands-Augustins

✆ 43 25 45 94

Ⓜ St-Michel métro

Open: Mon–Fri lunch and dinner, Sat–Sun dinner

Reservations essential

All credit cards accepted

French

€€

This casual bistro by the Seine is run by Michelin chef Guy Savoy and offers the chance to sample his style of cooking without taking out a bank loan. One *prix fixe* menu option is totally vegetarian. Try the mashed potatoes with olive oil.

La Closerie des Lilas

171 blvd du Montparnasse

✆ 40 51 34 50

Ⓜ Vavin métro or Port Royal RER

Open: brasserie daily from 1130, restaurant daily lunch and dinner

Reservations recommended for restaurant

All credit cards accepted

French

€€

Take a drink at the bar where the likes of Hemingway and Picasso drank, or dine in the casual brasserie or slightly more formal restaurant. The food is decent rather than special, but the steak tartare is recommended.

L'Épi Dupin ⑦

11 r. Dupin

✆ 42 22 64 56

Ⓜ Sèvres-Babylone métro

Open: Mon–Fri lunch and dinner; closed Christmas and three weeks in Aug

Reservations essential

American Express

French

€€

This fashionable and busy restaurant offers some of the best and most reasonably priced food in Paris, so book ahead. Try the cod with saffroned leek and leave room for one of their excellent desserts.

Jacques Cagna ⑧

14 r. des Grands-Augustins

✆ 43 26 49 39

Ⓜ Odéon métro

Open: Tue–Fri lunch and dinner, Mon and Sat dinner only

Reservations essential

All credit cards accepted

French haute cuisine

€€€

Old-fashioned dining room with superb cuisine from Michelin-rated chef Jacques Cagna. The fixed-price lunch menu is a bargain, but you'll need to go à la carte to sample the full complexity of dishes such as roast spring lamb with black olive polenta.

Lapérouse ⑨

51 quai des Grands-Augustins

✆ 43 26 68 04

Ⓜ St-Michel métro

Open: Mon–Fri lunch and dinner, Sat dinner; closed Aug

Reservations recommended

All credit cards accepted

French

€€€

Great location by the Seine and fabulous belle-époque dining rooms, many of which can be booked privately. All is matched by the impeccable cooking, with *quenelles* as a house speciality.

Le Relais Louis XIII

8 r. des Grands-Augustins

✆ 43 26 75 96

Ⓜ St-Michel métro

Open: Tue–Sat lunch and dinner, Mon dinner

Reservations recommended

American Express

French

€€€

This former monastery is now a gourmet restaurant, but with the ancient atmosphere preserved. Sea bass in a creamy herb sauce is one regular dish, and it is also noted for its excellent coffees, including Jamaican Blue Mountain, arguably the best in the world.

ST-GERMAIN
Bars, cafés and pubs

L'Assignat
7 r. Guénégaud
✆ 43 54 87 68
Ⓜ Mabillon métro
Open: Mon–Sat from 0900, hot meals at lunchtime, snacks all day; closed July
Reservations unnecessary
No credit cards accepted
€

The charm of this café-bar lies in its very ordinariness, making no concessions to fashion or tourism but providing a welcoming retreat for the local people, especially the many students in the area.

Brasserie Lipp
151 blvd St-Germain
✆ 45 48 53 91
Ⓜ St-Germain-des-Prés métro
Open: daily from 1130
Reservations recommended
All credit cards accepted
€€

From President Mitterrand to Sharon Stone, many famous names have eaten and continue to eat in this 130-year-old brasserie. Daily specials include a *cassoulet* on Thursdays, but with a wide range of fish and meat dishes too.

Café de Flore
172 blvd St-Germain
✆ 45 48 55 26
Ⓜ St-Germain-des-Prés métro
Open: daily from 0700
Reservations not allowed
All credit cards accepted
€€

The Left Bank wouldn't be the Left Bank without places such as this; Dalí and Picasso are just two of the famous names who drank and argued here. Snacks are available all day, but you could settle for a coffee, a croissant or a glass of wine.

Café de la Mairie
8 pl. St-Sulpice
✆ 43 26 67 82
Ⓜ St-Sulpice métro
Open: Mon–Sat from 0700, daily in June, food from 1130

Reservations unnecessary
No credit cards accepted
€

Overlooking the Église St-Sulpice, this old-fashioned café is a great place to retreat for a drink or a snack, and to take a break from sightseeing in the square where Catherine Deneuve lives.

Chez Georges

11 r. des Cannettes
⌀ 43 26 79 15
◉ Mabillon métro
Open: Tue–Sat from 1200; closed Aug
Reservations not allowed
No credit cards accepted
€

In an area packed with tourist haunts it's good to know of ordinary bars like this, with character, where you can get a feel for real Parisian life. There's sometimes music at weekends and simple food is available all day, along with beer, wine and coffee.

Le Comptoir du Relais

5 carrefour de l'Odéon
⌀ 43 29 12 05
◉ Odéon métro
Open: Mon–Sat from 1200, Sun from 1300; closed three weeks in Aug
Reservations unnecessary
No credit cards accepted
€

A wine bar with the emphasis firmly on the wine, although you can order an enjoyable range of basic foods throughout the day. Numerous wines are available by the glass, giving you a chance to experiment, and many French regional wines are represented. Great décor, with a tiled floor and mirrored walls.

Les Deux Magots

6 pl. St-Germain-des-Prés
⌀ 45 48 55 25
◉ St-Germain-des-Prés métro
Open: daily from 0730
Reservations not allowed
All credit cards accepted
€€

This former café haunt of Sartre and Samuel Beckett is now more geared to the passing tourists, but a visit is an almost essential part of the Parisian experience. Brasserie food is served all day, but most people content themselves with a coffee and watch the world go by.

L'Écluse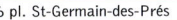

15 quai des Grands-Augustins
⌀ 46 33 58 74
◉ St-Michel métro
Open: daily from 1130
Reservations unnecessary
American Express
€€

This wine bar by the Seine is part of a chain but still manages to retain a character of its own: it's smart but relaxed. The food is better than average, too: wild mushrooms with ginger and nutmeg served in filo pastry, for example.

Le Lutétia

Hôtel Lutétia, 45 blvd Raspail
⌀ 49 54 46 46
◉ Sèvres-Babylone métro
Open: daily from 1100
Reservations not allowed
All credit cards accepted
€€

This hotel bar, open to non-residents, is a good place to know about if you want a relaxed drink in a more sophisticated and comfortable atmosphere. Cocktails, wines, beers and liqueurs are not cheap, but there is live jazz several nights a week.

La Palette

43 r. de Seine
⌀ 43 26 68 15
◉ Mabillon métro
Open: Mon–Sat from 0800, hot meals lunchtime only but snacks all day; closed three weeks in Aug
Reservations not allowed
VISA
€

This café scores for its wonderful belle-époque décor and artistic ambience, and while the food is nothing out of the ordinary, the setting and the atmosphere make this a great place to while away the time and make yourself feel Parisian, at least temporarily.

ST-GERMAIN
Shops, markets and picnic sites

Shops

Barthélémy (21)

51 r. de Grenelle

☎ 45 48 56 75

Ⓜ Rue de Bac métro

Open: Tue–Sat 0700–1930

This terrific cheese shop in the food-conscious rue de Bac area has hundreds of French cheeses from familiar bries and camemberts to more unusual varieties from regions that are lesser-known to visitors. Cheeseboards and other kitchen items are also available.

Cacao et Chocolat (22)

29 r. de Buci

☎ 46 33 77 63

Ⓜ Mabillon métro

Open: Tue–Sat 1030–1930

All credit cards accepted

While there are countless fine chocolate shops in Paris, many look very similar and stock similar items, but here you can buy unusual flavours such as honey and chilli pepper, and the smart wooden boxes in which the chocolates are packed make great presents to take home.

Charcuterie Alsacienne (23)

10 r. de Buci

☎ 43 54 93 49

Ⓜ St-Germain-des-Prés métro

Open: daily 0930–2000

If visiting the rue de Buci market don't miss this Alsace specialist shop which stocks the best produce from the region, including prepared meats, cakes, wines and liqueurs. Sausages abound – try pork with cumin.

Charcuterie Charles (24)

10 r. Dauphine

☎ 43 54 25 19

Ⓜ Odéon métro

Open: Mon–Fri 0830–1400 and 1600–2000

A treasure trove of prepared meats and a sausage lover's heaven, with dozens of exotic varieties, their *boudin blanc* (white pork and veal) has won awards, and comes with truffles, prunes and other flavours.

Charcuterie Coesnon (25)

30 r. Dauphine

☎ 43 54 35 80

Ⓜ Odéon métro

Open: Tue–Sat 0830–1900

Run by a family from Normandy, this stocks the best of that region's wonderful produce, most notably a range of homemade sausages including *andouillettes*, pâtés, *foie gras*, hams and other meaty delights.

Jean-Paul Hévin (30)

3 r. Vavin

☎ 43 54 09 85

Ⓜ Vavin métro

Open: daily, closed Sun lunch and all day Sun in Jul–Aug

One of the stars of the world of chocolate-making, which is taken very seriously in Paris (*see page 46*). The taste can be too rich for some, so try his *palets amers* first, small squares of bitter chocolate.

Jean-Pierre Carton 26

6 r. de Buci

✆ 43 26 04 13

Odéon métro

Open: Tue–Sun all day

You might be forgiven for mistaking this bakery for a patisserie as the window is full of such tempting delights as lemon and chocolate tarts, but you can also buy bread rolls filled with olives, bacon or other mouth-watering options.

Olivier & Co 27

28 r. de Buci

✆ 44 07 15 43

St-Germain-des-Prés métro

Open: Mon 1430–1930, Tue–Sun 1030–1930

 American Express

This specialist in olive oil offers tastings from the 15 main oils that it sells – all from six different countries including France, Italy and Spain.

Poilâne 19

8 r. du Cherche-Midi

✆ 45 48 42 59

Sèvres-Babylone or St-Sulpice métro

Open: Mon–Sat 0715–2015

No credit cards accepted

One name stands head and shoulders above all others in the serious world of French bread, and that is Lionel Poilâne. His *pain Poilâne* is a huge oval, thankfully also available in halves or quarters. Many cafés and haute cuisine restaurants boast on their menus that they use bread by Poilâne, and in his surprisingly tiny shop here is your chance to buy some for picnics or to take home.

Markets

Marché Biologique 28

Blvd Raspail

Sèvres-Babylone métro

Open: Sun

Much French produce sold in markets is organic without being labelled as such, but in this weekly outlet the farmers who pride themselves on the purity of their foodstuffs display their wares, including wines, meats, vegetables, fruit, cheeses, mushrooms, bread and many other items too.

Rue de Buci market 29

R. de Buci and r. de Seine

Odéon or Mabillon métro

Open: Mon–Sat all day and Sun am

Picasso did his shopping here in one of the more up-market markets, with huge stalls crammed with fresh fruit and veg filling the streets. Don't forget to check the shops either side of the streets too, where many specialist food stores can be found, stocking rich sources of regional fare, wines, cheeses, cold meats, bread and patisseries.

Choice chocolate

Aphrodisiac, medicine or indulgence?

Chocolate shops are as much a part of the Paris scene as the Eiffel Tower, although they have been around a lot longer. The first was opened as long ago as 1659 in the rue de l'Arbre Sec, and it was a royal affair. Chocolate had reached Europe in the 17th century and was in great demand, and **King Louis XIV** granted one of Queen Anne's officers the exclusive right to sell chocolate in Paris. It was first available only as a drink, but just as might happen today there was a great debate over whether this new foodstuff was good for you, or potentially dangerous. Chocolate tasted so good that people wondered if it was an aphrodisiac and no doubt the importers and sellers were happy to encourage them to think that.

By the early 19th century it was actually being sold as a medicine by two enterprising Parisians. Monsieur Debauve was one of the city's first chocolatiers, and his partner Monsieur Gallais was a pharmacist. Just how they knew it would cure assorted ailments isn't known, but it was the start of a successful partnership and today there are several **Debauve & Gallais** chocolate shops around the city, but they no longer need to persuade people that chocolate will cure their ills.

One of the most famous Parisian chocolatiers these days is **Jean-Paul Hévin** (*see pages 44 and 54*), winner of the highly coveted award as Meilleur Ouvrier de France (Best Worker in France). Such is his renown that the chef-*pâtissier* at London's Savoy Hotel goes all the way to Hévin's little shop in Paris to source some of his supplies. He must find it hard to choose, as almost everything looks tempting, and you feel you want to sample just one of each and every type before buying. However, the reverential air that suggests something between a jewellery store and a designer boutique means that such wishes will not be indulged. Try the raspberry truffle, or one steeped in alcohol, for a mouth-watering sensation.

Equally famous is **Christian Constant** (*see page 51*), whose quest for new combinations and flavours takes him all over the world. Here, next to the shop, is a tiny tearoom where you can sample a range of hot chocolate drinks concocted by Monsieur Constant, along with a variety of pastries which show the effects of the chocolatier's travels. How

about Fleur de China, a combination of chocolate, crème brûlée, green tea and jasmine? In all there are 36 kinds of tea, not to mention five types of sugar, and the most popular purchase of all, which is a simple bittersweet chocolate bar.

Such is the seriousness with which Paris regards its chocolate that chocolate lovers have got together and formed a club with the grand title of the '**Club des Croqueurs de Chocolat**'. The members meet frequently to assess the latest creations from the city's chocolate makers.

Despite their apparent obsession with chocolate, the French eat less of it than their European neighbours: the Swiss devour 23 pounds of chocolate per head of population per year, while the Belgians – another great chocolate-making nation – manage just 19 pounds. The French eat 15 pounds a year, just ahead of the Americans who munch their way through 12 pounds of it.

Try the raspberry truffle, or one steeped in alcohol, for a mouth-watering sensation.

Visitors to Paris who are only familiar with commercial chocolate bars, mainly of milk chocolate, should be warned that their tastebuds are going to be seriously assaulted when first trying a good French chocolate. To begin with, it will almost certainly be dark, not milk, and even if you have tried regular dark chocolate it is a whole new experience to bite into a bar or an individual chocolate that has a far higher cacao content than you are used to. It will be like someone who only has one small glass of sherry a year suddenly being given pure alcohol. The Parisians also like their chocolate bittersweet rather than sweet, so that too can be a shock to the system, although in the case of most visitors it is a very pleasant shock indeed. The French may not have invented chocolate, but they have certainly refined it in their inimitable fashion to make it one of the great taste sensations of the city.

The Eiffel Tower and Les Invalides

The area stretching from the Eiffel Tower to Les Invalides, where Napoleon is buried, is one of the most prosperous in the city, a fact reflected in its many expensive restaurants, popular with businessmen and diplomats. There are cheaper options too, and one of the most in-demand eating places in Paris: the Jules Verne restaurant, actually in the Eiffel Tower itself.

THE EIFFEL TOWER AND LES INVALIDES
Restaurants

L'Affriolé

17 r. Malar

⌀ 44 18 31 33

La Tour Maubourg or Invalides métro

Open: Mon–Fri lunch and dinner, Sat dinner

Reservations essential

French

€€

The locals are lucky to have this bright place as their neighbourhood bistro, where the food is way ahead of standard bistro fare without being overly expensive. Rabbit stuffed with mushrooms, artichokes and *foie gras* is just one example.

L'Arpège

84 r. de Varenne

⌀ 45 51 47 33

Varenne métro

Open: Mon–Fri lunch and dinner

Reservations essential

All credit cards accepted

French haute cuisine

€€€

If money is no object choose the chef's tasting menu for several courses showing off Alain Passard's distinguished skills, with langoustine carpaccio with caviar being a speciality. Try the unique twelve-flavoured tomato dessert too.

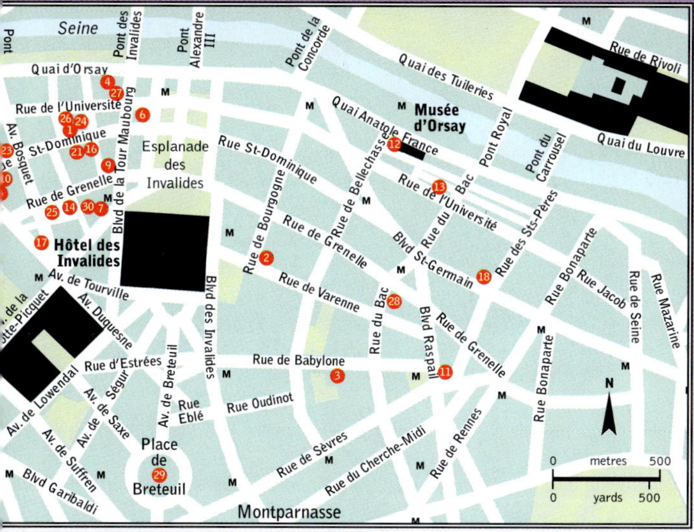

La Bamboche ❸

15 r. de Babylone

✆ 45 49 14 40

Ⓜ Sèvres-Babylone métro

Open: Mon–Fri lunch and dinner

Reservations recommended

💳 VISA

French

€€

Chic and not cheap, this restaurant does offer one inexpensive and one pricier *prix fixe* menu, with dishes ranging from a simple grilled salmon or steak to the more challenging calf's head, a chef's special.

Le Bar au Sel ❹

49 quai d'Orsay

✆ 45 51 58 58

Ⓜ Invalides métro or RER

Open: daily lunch and dinner

Reservations recommended

All credit cards accepted

French-Seafood

€€

Stylish seafood restaurant which is not too expensive given the quality on offer, and dishes include the house speciality, after which it is named, sea bass cooked in a salt crust.

Le Bourdonnais ❺

113 av. de la Bourdonnais

✆ 47 05 47 96

Ⓜ École Militaire métro

Open: daily lunch and dinner

Reservations essential

💳 VISA American Express

French

€€€

This is serious French dining for those who love elaborate food and flavours, so abandon worries about the waistband for a while. Lobster sautéed with chestnuts and served with Swiss chard crêpes is one Bourdonnais dish.

Le Divellec ❻

107 r. de l'Université

✆ 45 51 91 96

Ⓜ Invalides métro

Open: Mon–Sat lunch and dinner; closed Christmas

Reservations recommended

All credit cards accepted

French-Seafood

€€€

▲ The Eiffel Tower

Elegant décor with a distinct nautical theme combines with attentive service in this seafood specialist eatery. Be prepared for fine fish dishes such as cod with grains of caviar or mussels with shallots, and an impressive dessert trolley.

Écaille et Plume

25 r. Duvivier

⌀ 45 55 06 72

🚇 École Militaire métro

Open: Mon–Fri lunch and dinner, Sat dinner

Reservations essential

💳 💳 American Express

French

€€

Game is the speciality of this family-run restaurant, with partridge, grouse, boar and venison all featuring when in season. Dishes are prepared with a light touch, though, by the owner's wife in the kitchen, but it is suggested that vegetarians should phone in advance for a special menu.

Jules Verne ❽

Second level of the Eiffel Tower, Champ de Mars

⌀ 45 55 61 44

🚇 Champ de Mars Tour Eiffel RER or Bir-Hakeim métro

Open: daily lunch and dinner

Reservations essential

All credit cards accepted

French haute cuisine-Fusion

€€€

There can be no finer location to dine in than looking out from the Eiffel Tower, but the food here is excellent too. The focus is French cooking (such as a terrine of leeks, truffles and *foie gras*) but there are occasional menus featuring world cuisine.

Paul Minchelli ❾

54 blvd de la Tour Maubourg

⌀ 47 05 89 86

🚇 La Tour Maubourg métro

Open: Tue–Sat lunch and dinner; closed Aug, Christmas and New Year

Reservations recommended

💳 💳

French-Seafood

€€€

This elegant fish restaurant appeals to well-heeled Parisians. The cooking style is simple, concentrating on the taste of the fish rather than fancy sauces – try scallops cooked in their shells or skate fin in tarragon vinegar.

Le Violon d'Ingres

135 r. St-Dominique

⌀ 45 55 15 05

🚇 Pont de l'Alma RER or École Militaire métro

Open: Tue–Sat lunch and dinner; closed three weeks in July/Aug and at Christmas

Reservations essential

All credit cards accepted

French

€€€

Star chef **Christian Constant** opened this bistro in 1997, but don't expect bistro fare or prices. A *prix fixe* lunch menu is the best value with à la carte dishes including such things as sea bass on a bed of spinach and garnished with capers.

Le Divellec

« *La cuisine de la Mer* »

THE EIFFEL TOWER AND LES INVALIDES
Bars, cafés and pubs

Au Sauvignon

80 r. des Sts-Péres

∅ 45 48 49 02

Sèvres-Babylone métro

Open: Mon–Sat from 0830; closed Aug

Reservations unnecessary

If all you want is a glass of wine and a simple cold meal, then try this wine bar where the owner rotates the dozen or so wines that are available by the glass, with of course many more for sale by the bottle. Cold meats, cheeses and salads are available all day, but there are no hot meals.

Café des Hauteurs

Musée d'Orsay

∅ 45 49 42 33

Musée d'Orsay RER or Solférino métro

Open: Tue–Sun 1000–1700

No credit cards accepted

This delightful rooftop café in this must-see museum tends to be busy as it's right by the number one attraction: the Impressionists. The design is fabulous, with a view out across the city through one of the old railway clocks. It serves tea, coffee, wine, beer and light snacks such as sandwiches and cakes.

Café des Lettres

53 r. de Verneuil

∅ 42 22 52 17

Rue de Bac métro

Open: Mon–Sat from 0900, Sun lunchtime only; closed Christmas and New Year

Reservations unnecessary

Scandinavian and seafood dishes predominate in this café-cum-bar, thanks to the Swedish owner, and there's a lovely open courtyard in which to eat them or to just sit with a glass of wine or a coffee.

Café du Marché

38 r. Cler

∅ 47 05 51 27

École Militaire métro

Open: daily from 0700, food Mon–Sat 1130–2300, Sun lunch only

Reservations unnecessary

A handy place to take a break from the rue Cler market, along with many other shoppers, and sit at pavement tables on a pleasant traffic-free street. There's a good choice of salads, sandwiches and simple snacks, or sip a coffee or a glass of wine.

Café le Dôme

41 av. de la Bourdonnais

∅ 45 51 45 41

Pont de l'Alma RER or École Militaire métro

Open: daily from 0700, food from 1200

Reservations unnecessary

With its views of the Eiffel Tower, this unassuming little café-brasserie has a good beer list as well as wine list, and the menu includes a range of salads from all over France, including a *salade niçoise* and *salade lyonnaise*.

Café Thoumieux

4 av. de la Comète

∅ 45 51 50 40

La Tour-Maubourg métro

Open: Mon–Fri from 1200, Sat from 1700; closed first two weeks in Aug

Reservations unnecessary

 American Express

Eclectic café-bar serving French bistro food at

52 | The Eiffel Tower and Les Invalides

lunchtime, with Spanish *tapas* taking over in the evening. The plush décor combines with a large cocktail list to suggest sophistication, yet there is large-screen TV offering sport too.

Master's Bar

64 av. Bosquet
✆ 45 51 08 99
Ⓜ École Militaire métro
Open: daily from 1700; closed part of Aug
Reservations not allowed

This is a basic bar with a rather bizarre appeal – you might wander in on one of their unannounced theme nights – though otherwise it's a great place for people-watching as well as sampling the extensive cocktail list which allows the bartenders to show off their skills.

Le Rouquet

188 blvd St-Germain
✆ 45 48 06 93
Ⓜ St-Germain-des-Prés métro
Open: Mon–Sat 0700–2100, hot meals lunchtime only
Reservations unnecessary

Lacking the historical and artistic connections of other cafés on the boulevard, Le Rouquet makes up for it with its simplicity, cheaper prices, all-day snacks and simple lunches, plus a sheltered seating area giving a good view on to the boulevard.

Sancerre

22 av. Rapp
✆ 45 51 75 91
Ⓜ École Militaire or Alma-Marceau métro
Open: Mon–Fri 0830–2130, Sat 0830–1630; closed first three weeks in Aug

This unpretentious little wine bar has a relaxed feel and features both décor and wines from the vineyards and village of Sancerre. If there is a wine you particularly like, they also sell bottles to take away. There is also a small outside seating terrace.

▲ Hôtel des Invalides

The Eiffel Tower and Les Invalides | 53

THE EIFFEL TOWER AND LES INVALIDES
Shops, markets and picnic sites

Shops

L'Ambassade du Sud-Ouest 20

46 av. de la Bourdonnais
✆ 45 55 59 59
Ⓜ École Militaire métro
Open: daily 1000–2300; closed one week in Aug

Southwest France has some of the heartiest and meatiest produce in the country, and here's where you can get it if you want a picnic lunch for the nearby gardens. Try a country pâté and something sweet like an apple tart.

Androuet 21

83 r. St-Dominique
✆ 45 50 45 75
Ⓜ La Tour-Maubourg métro
Open: Tue–Sat 0800–2030 and Mon pm

The Androuet family has been selling cheese in Paris since 1909 and now has several shops, this one being particularly well stocked and, being on the Left Bank, the staff are used to dealing with overseas visitors asking about the cheeses.

Desgrippes 22

16 av. Rapp
✆ 45 51 66 39
Ⓜ École Militaire or Pont de l'Alma métro
Open: Mon–Sat 0715–2000; closed Aug

If you want to sit in the gardens and have a picnic after visiting the Eiffel Tower, pop along to this bakery and pastry shop and stock up on fresh baguettes, croissants, cakes, filled rolls or one of their specialities, *raissol aux pruneaux*, a pastry stuffed with prunes.

Duchesne 23

112 r. St-Dominique
✆ 45 51 31 01
Ⓜ École Militaire or Pont de l'Alma métro
Open: Mon–Sat 0730–2000; closed July or Aug
No credit cards accepted

Not many pastry shops have chandeliers hanging from the ceiling and walls covered in mosaics, so buying here is as much a pleasure as eating afterwards – and that will be considerable if you take away some freshly baked rolls and a chocolate mousse cake with orange.

Jean-Luc Poujauran 24

20 r. Jean Nicot
✆ 47 05 80 88
Ⓜ La Tour-Maubourg métro
Open: Mon–Sat 0830–2030
No credit cards accepted

This bakery claims to have been the first in Paris to produce an organic baguette, and now supplies hundreds of restaurants with their bread.

Jean-Paul Hévin 7

16 av. de la Motte Picquet

✆ 45 51 77 48

◉ La Tour-Maubourg métro

Open: Tue–Sat, closed three weeks in Aug

Renowned chocolate-maker Hévin's second shop, which like the first (*see page 44*) is as much a jewellery store or gallery, and as well as a vast array of chocolates also carries cakes, croissants, teas, coffees and lunchtime sandwiches.

Marie-Anne Cantin 25

12 r. du Champ-de-Mars

✆ 45 50 43 94

◉ École Militaire métro

Open: Tue–Sat 0830–1300 and 1600–1930, Sun 0830–1300

American Express

This immaculate cheese shop stocks about a hundred varieties, and many of them are bought in young, then aged to perfection in the cellars beneath the shop.

Michel Chaudin 26

149 r. de l'Université

✆ 47 53 74 40

◉ Invalides métro

Open: Tue–Sat 0930–1930; closed Aug

This shop is a chocoholic's dream, being packed with some of the most tempting creations you will ever see. The owner is noted for his bittersweet truffles, called *esmereldas*, and for rich chocolate cakes.

Petrossian 27

18 blvd de La Tour Maubourg

✆ 44 11 32 22

◉ La Tour-Maubourg or Invalides métro

Open: Tue–Fri 0900–2000, Mon and Sat 0930–2000; closed Mondays in Aug

American Express

This family shop specialises in produce from Russia and some of its former republics, such as Georgia, the first country in the world to make wine. Caviar and vodka feature (naturally!), with Russian breads and pastries also available if you want to have a snack.

Ryst-Dupeyron 28

79 r. du Bac

✆ 45 48 80 93

◉ Rue du Bac métro

Open: Tue–Sat 1030–1930, Mon 1230–1930; closed the week of Aug 15

This area is rich in food shops and here is the wine shop to match, if you want to track down a rare wine or brandy. They also sell whisky and other spirits, some of the best French liqueurs, and there are plenty of inexpensive wines on offer too.

 Markets

Breteuil Market 29

Av. de Saxe/pl. de Breteuil

◉ Ségur métro

Open: Thu and Sat

The archetypal Parisian market with the Eiffel Tower visible in the background and many excellent food stalls in amongst the clothing and other goods for sale. One stall alone boasts 38 varieties of apples. With almost 200 stands, it is one of the city's biggest, and has been going since 1873.

Rue Cler Market 30

Rue Cler

◉ École Militaire métro

Open: Tue–Sat and Sun

This is a more up-market market than most, in a smart neighbourhood where there are already many fine food shops. It is also on a wide traffic-free street, but don't get so absorbed in the market that you miss the shops either side, especially the Italian shop **Davoli** (*34 r. Cler*).

 Picnic sites

Parc du Champ de Mars 31

The Eiffel Tower is on everyone's itinerary and the best approach is from across the river, but when you get there you might want to allow time for a picnic in the grounds beyond the Tower, the Parc du Champ de Mars. There are plenty of pathways and seats and no shortage of nearby shops where you can put together a mouth-watering picnic lunch.

Family eating

Treats for all the family

To take children to the gourmet capital of the world might seem to be asking for trouble, yet it is in fact perfectly possible to travel there with children and have a great time. That said, you will have to sacrifice the great meals in the gourmet temples unless you can organise babysitters, which is easy to do through organisations such as **Inter-Service Parents** (∅ *44 93 44 93*) and **Kid's Service** (∅ *47 66 00 52*).

There are plenty of attractions to interest children, and no youngsters would complain at being forced to eat ice cream at **Berthillon** (*see page 24*) which the parents can also regard as a great food experience. There are plenty of chocolate shops too, which will appeal to young and old alike, though children might not share the French taste for rich chocolate.

Paris is filled with parks where children can play, many of them having specific playground areas where the parents need only sit and supervise, fortified by a picnic lunch put together at one of the markets, bakers, delicatessens or other food shops around Paris.

When it comes to actually sitting down and eating together, most Parisian restaurants are perfectly welcoming to children, with the obvious exceptions of the more formal places, where the food and experience would be wasted on children anyway. That said, eating out in the evenings is not quite the family affair in France that it is in, say, Italy or Greece, so you might want to choose somewhere that specifically caters for children.

There are two restaurant chains that cater especially well for families, with about thirty branches of each throughout the city, so look for a **Bistro Romain** or the bright signs for the **Hippo** chain. Both have junior menus as well as decent choices for the adults too, and this being Paris the parents won't be expected to drink Coke or Fanta just because that's what their children want. Hippo restaurants also provide

colouring books and feature video screens showing cartoons to hold the kids' attention while the adults chat and eat.

Paris naturally also has countless branches of **McDonald's**, **Burger King** and the various pizza parlours, plus other fast food favourites, including the **Hard Rock Café** (*see page 73*) for older children, if they insist on being unadventurous. You could try to coax them into putting together a rather more healthy sandwich in a bakery or from a street stall, especially if you combine it with a visit to a patisserie for chocolate cakes or strawberry tarts.

One place that caters especially well for children is **Chicago Meatpackers** (*8 r. Coquillière; ⌀ 40 28 02 33; open: daily from 1130; reservations unnecessary;* ⬤ 🟦 *American Express;* ⓢ). It's the kind of place where kids are allowed to behave as kids do – wandering away from the table, scribbling on the menu, talking constantly. It's an American beef and burgers kind of a place, but the quality is good and adults might want to opt for the spicier Tex-Mex end of the menu and the wines from California. The waiters all speak English and have the patience of saints. There's a clown show every hour and longer bouts of entertainment on Wednesday, Saturday and Sunday.

Somewhere else that lays on the entertainment is **Justine**

▲ Hippo restaurant

(*Méridien-Montparnasse Hotel, 19 r. du Commandant-Mouchotte; ⌀ 44 36 44 00*) which is free for the under-4s and offers face painting, dancing and competitions organised by the bubbly staff every Sunday, leaving the parents free to enjoy the food. Combine sightseeing with eating and dine at **Altitude 95** (*First floor, Eiffel Tower; ⌀ 45 55 20 04*), which also has entertainment provided, along with an inexpensive *prix fixe* menu for young children (it includes a gift for everyone when they leave). The location is great and you can call in after taking the lift to the top of the tower.

> **Justine offers face painting, dancing and competitions organised by the bubbly staff every Sunday, leaving the parents free to enjoy the food.**

The Champs-Elysées, the Arc de Triomphe and St-Honoré

This is where the famous names are, from the long-established Maxim's to two of Paris's best contemporary chefs: Alain Ducasse and Guy Savoy. It is also the part of the city where you'll find top-notch food shops, whose window displays are works of art guaranteed to make you want to buy.

THE CHAMPS-ELYSÉES, THE ARC DE TRIOMPHE AND ST-HONORÉ
Restaurants

Alain Ducasse ❶

59 av. Raymond-Poincaré
☏ 47 27 12 27
Ⓜ Victor Hugo métro

Open: Mon–Fri lunch and dinner; closed mid-July–mid-Aug, Christmas and New Year
Reservations essential
All credit cards accepted
French haute cuisine

€€€

The finest French food from the first chef ever to earn six Michelin stars: three here and three at **Le Louis XV** in Monaco. Expensive but a sublime eating experience, against which you are likely to judge all future meals. The truffle soup is just one heavenly dish that you can try.

Les Ambassadeurs ❷

Hôtel de Crillon, 10 pl. de la Concorde
☏ 44 71 16 16
Ⓜ Concorde métro

Open: daily lunch and dinner
Reservations essential
All credit cards accepted
French haute cuisine

€€€

Worth it for the dining room alone, a spectacular glass-and-marble space that overlooks the place de la Concorde. The food is equal to the setting: smoked salmon with whipped cream and caviar is one speciality on offer.

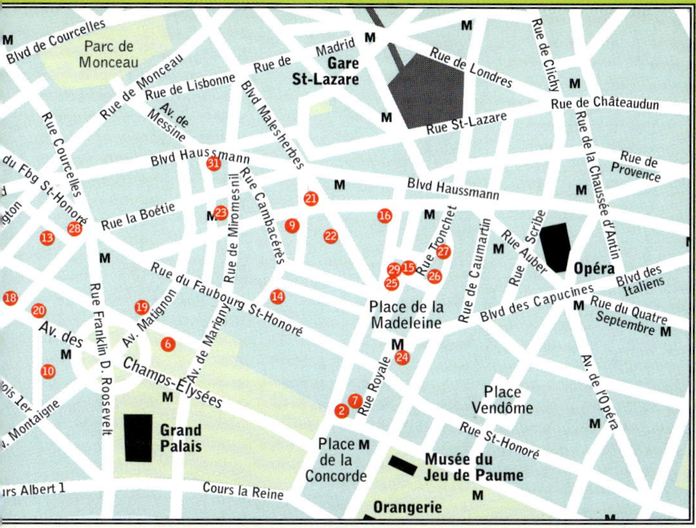

The Champs-Elysées, the Arc de Triomphe and St-Honoré | 59

Le Cinq ❸

George V Hotel, 31 av. George V

∅ 53 53 28 00

◉ George V métro

Open: daily lunch and dinner

Reservations recommended

All credit cards accepted

French

€€€

The sophisticated new restaurant in the luxury George V Hotel is both reverential towards the food but relaxed in atmosphere. Sautéed lobster perfumed with pepper and mango is an exceptional dish.

Guy Savoy ❹

18 r. Troyon

∅ 43 80 40 61

◉ Charles de Gaulle-Étoile métro

Open: Mon–Fri lunch and dinner, Sat dinner

Reservations essential

American Express

French haute cuisine

€€€

One of the chefs who sets the standards, Guy Savoy presents the best contemporary French cuisine, from artichoke and truffle soup through to lemon tart on a pineapple compote. Think of the experience, not the price.

Le Jardin ❺

Hôtel Royal Monceau, 37 av. Hoche

∅ 42 99 98 70

▲ Guy Savoy

🌐 Charles de Gaulle-Étoile métro

| Open: Mon–Fri lunch and dinner |
| Reservations essential |
| All credit cards accepted |
| French |
| €€€ |

As a hotel restaurant Le Jardin is not as well known as some of the star names, but it can easily hold its own for cuisine. A courtyard setting enhances the food, of which duck with pine kernels and lemons is one signature dish.

Laurent

| 41 av. Gabriel |
| ✆ 42 25 00 39 |
| 🌐 Champs-Elysées-Clemenceau métro |
| Open: Mon–Fri lunch and dinner, Sat dinner |
| Reservations essential |
| All credit cards accepted |
| French haute cuisine |
| €€€ |

Another Parisian gastronomic temple in an area that overflows with them, Laurent offers a grandly old-fashioned dining room but exquisite modern cooking: spring lamb basted in honey and thyme is just one fine example.

Maxim's 7

| 3 r. Royale |
| ✆ 42 65 27 94 |
| 🌐 Concorde métro |
| Open: Mon–Sat lunch and dinner; closed Mon in July/Aug |
| Reservations essential |
| All credit cards accepted |
| French |
| €€€ |

Maxim's is a name synonymous with Parisian glitz and glamour, and that is what you pay for here rather than the food, which is better elsewhere. Art-nouveau décor, and an orchestra, are all part of the package, with sautéed duck *foie gras* in a blackcurrant sauce a part of the menu.

Pierre Gagnaire 8

| 6 r. Balzac |
| ✆ 44 35 18 25 |
| 🌐 George V métro |
| Open: Mon–Fri lunch and dinner, Sun dinner; closed mid-July–mid-Aug |
| Reservations essential |
| All credit cards accepted |
| French haute cuisine |
| €€€ |

One of the best – and priciest – places in Paris, but worth every franc; there are several *prix fixe* menus to suit various budgets, but go à la carte for incomparable dishes such as pan-fried turbot with mixed spices.

Le Restaurant de l'Astor

| Hôtel Astor, 11 r. d'Astorg |
| ✆ 53 05 05 20 |
| 🌐 St-Augustin métro |
| Open: Mon–Fri lunch and dinner; closed Aug |
| Reservations recommended |
| All credit cards accepted |
| French |
| €€€ |

food & wine

Formal dining in a contemporary setting, with some *prix fixe* menus offering the chance to sample such dishes as warm *foie gras* with lentils, all without breaking the bank. Leave space for the sumptuous desserts, such as chocolate or lemon tart.

Spoon, Food and Wine

| 14 r. de Marignan |
| ✆ 40 76 34 44 |
| 🌐 Franklin D Roosevelt métro |
| Open: Mon–Fri lunch and dinner; closed three weeks July/Aug |
| Reservations essential |
| All credit cards accepted |
| French |
| €€ |

A bold venture by gourmet chef Alain Ducasse, serving exemplary food from around the world at affordable prices. Choose your own combination of main dish, sauce and side dish, or go for the chef's recommendation.

The Champs-Elysées, the Arc de Triomphe and St-Honoré | 61

THE CHAMPS-ELYSÉES, THE ARC DE TRIOMPHE AND ST-HONORÉ
Bars, cafés and pubs

Bar des Théatres ⓫

6 av. Montaigne
∅ 47 23 34 63
Ⓜ Alma-Marceau métro
Open: daily from 0600, hot meals from 1200
Reservations unnecessary
💳 VISA American Express
☕☕

In an expensive area not well served by cafés, this is a terrific one to know about, with a separate brasserie too, for a more substantial meal. It appeals to shoppers trawling the nearby designer outlets, and in the evenings to the theatregoers (and afterwards the actors) from the Comédie Theatre opposite.

Barfly ⓬

49 av. George V
∅ 53 67 84 60
Ⓜ George V métro
Open: Sun–Fri lunchtime and evenings, Sat evenings only
Reservations recommended
💳 VISA American Express
☕☕☕

The bar in which to see and be seen, if you can get past the picky doormen and be allowed into the exclusive set. Businessmen, models, actors and playboys all congregate here, making Barfly an experience, though not one you may want to repeat.

The Bowler ⓭

13 r. d'Artois
∅ 45 61 16 60
Ⓜ St-Phillipe du Roule métro
Open: daily from 1100, food Mon–Sat lunchtime and evenings, Sun 1200–1800
Reservations not allowed
💳 VISA American Express
☕

This English pub is actually as popular with local people as with visitors and ex-pats, with its cricket memorabilia and English pub grub such as fish and chips and beef in ale. With draught ale and TV sport, it makes for a lively if un-Parisian night out.

Bugsy's ⓮

15 r. Montalivet
∅ 42 68 18 44
Ⓜ Champs-Élysées-Clemenceau métro
Open: daily from 1200, food lunchtime only
Reservations not allowed
💳 VISA American Express
☕☕

Bugsy as in Bugsy Malone signifies the gangster theme of this smart place, which has a huge bar that is both well-tended and well-stocked with beers, wines and cocktails. A sophisticated but not expensive venue for a night's drinking.

Café Madeleine ⓯

1 r. Tronchet
∅ 42 65 21 91
Ⓜ Madeleine métro
Open: daily from 0730, food all day
Reservations unnecessary
All credit cards accepted
☕☕

Right on the place de la Madeleine, the open-air seating makes a good place to take a break from sampling the upmarket food shops all around, if you don't mind the noise of the traffic. Save your appetite for snacks from the shops, and use this place for a coffee and a rest.

The Cricketer ⓰

41 r. des Mathurins
∅ 40 07 01 45
Ⓜ St-Augustin métro
Open: daily from 1100, food lunchtime only but till 1800 at weekends
Reservations not allowed
💳 VISA
☕

Following the success of the **Bowler** (*see page 62*), the **Cricketer** offers the same jovial mix of draught English ale (from Adnam's in Suffolk), pub grub, sport on TV, pub games and a mix of Parisians and ex-pats who have made it their local.

Le Fouquet's

99 av. des Champs-Élysées

✆ 47 23 70 60

Ⓜ George V

Open: daily from 0800, food lunchtime and evenings

Reservations not allowed

All credit cards accepted

€€

Glamorous red and gold colours let you know that this is a much more sophisticated place to stop for a coffee on the Champs-Élysées than the red and yellow of McDonald's. You'll pay highly for the old-world atmosphere, though.

Montecristo Café

68 av. des Champs-Élysées

✆ 45 62 30 86

Ⓜ Franklin D Roosevelt métro

Open: daily from 1100, food all day

Reservations not allowed

All credit cards accepted

€€

This Cuban-style hangout is where to head if you want a late night on the town, drinking cuba libres and salsa-dancing the night away. There's a separate restaurant serving Caribbean food, with a large bar and music down in the basement.

Villa Barclay

3 av. Matignon

✆ 53 89 18 91

Ⓜ Franklin D Roosevelt métro

Open: Mon–Fri from 1200, Sat–Sun from 1500, food lunchtime and evenings

Reservations not allowed

All credit cards accepted

€€€

This sophisticated and expensive bar just off the Champs-Élysées attracts a chic and well-heeled crowd of glamorous young (and not-so-young) Parisians, and while the noise-level is high, so too is the comfort, with warm colours and relaxing sofas.

Virgin Café

2nd Floor, Virgin Megastore, 52 av. des Champs-Élysées

✆ 49 53 50 00

Ⓜ Franklin D Roosevelt métro

Open: Mon–Sat from 1000, Sun from 1200, food all day

Reservations not allowed

American Express

€€

This café has made a reputation for itself whether you want to shop in the store or not. It's a relaxing place with good views over the street, and surprisingly tasty food makes it a lunchtime option too, in an area where there are lots of over-priced places.

THE CHAMPS-ELYSÉES, THE ARC DE TRIOMPHE AND ST-HONORÉ
Shops, markets and picnic sites

Shops

Albert Menes ㉑

41 blvd Malesherbes
☏ 42 66 95 63
Ⓜ St-Augustin métro
Open: Tue–Sat 1000–1900, Mon 1400–1900; closed mid-July–mid-Aug
American Express

This unusual shop deals only in old-fashioned items, many of which are hard to get elsewhere, and its stock includes many traditionally made jams and other preserves (including a garlic preserve), as well as vinegars, biscuits and sauces.

Betjamen & Barton ㉒

23 blvd Malesherbes
☏ 42 65 86 17
Ⓜ Madeleine métro
Open: Mon–Sat 0930–1900; closed Sat in Aug
American Express

The very English name indicates a very English shop, with sweets and biscuits but especially tea – they claim almost 200 varieties, from conventional teas such as Darjeeling and Earl Grey to more exotic herbal teas, and even more exotic teapots.

La Bonbonnière Saint-Honoré ㉓

25 r. de Miromesnil
☏ 42 65 02 39
Ⓜ Miromesnil métro
Open: Mon–Fri 1000–1900

This chocolatier-cum-sweetshop sells a range of jams and preserves as well as biscuits, unusual sweets from the French regions, and of course a host of chocolates, from individual truffles to larger bars and gift boxes.

Boutique Maille ㉔

6 pl. de la Madeleine
☏ 40 15 06 00
Ⓜ Madeleine métro
Open: Mon–Sat 1000–1900

A heaven for mustard-lovers, Maille is a manufacturer of some of the finest mustards in France, and this small shop is its retail outlet. Its Dijon mustard is renowned, but if you want to be more adventurous there are dozens of flavoured mustards too ... cognac, perhaps?

Caviar Kaspia ㉕

17 pl. de la Madeleine
☏ 42 65 33 32
Ⓜ Madeleine métro
Open: Mon–Sat 1000–0100; closed one week in Aug
All credit cards accepted

The speciality here is obviously caviar, from around the world, plus serving and storage items, but other affiliated products too, such as smoked salmon and smoked eels, while an upstairs restaurant allows you to sample the products while relaxing.

Fauchon 26

26 and 28–30 pl. de la Madeleine
☏ 47 42 60 11
Ⓜ Madeleine métro
Open: Mon–Sat 0940–1900
All credit cards accepted

If you only have time to visit one food shop in Paris, make it this one. Its sumptuous window displays will have your mouth watering before you even step inside to examine the fish, exotic fruit, wines, vegetables, spices, coffee, tea, cheeses, pastries and fantastic salads and other ready-made dishes from the delicatessen.

La Ferme St-Hubert 27

21 r. Vignon
☏ 47 42 79 20
Ⓜ Madeleine métro
Open: Mon–Sat 0900–2000
American Express

Just off that food-lover's nirvana, the place de la Madeleine, is this small but well-stocked cheese shop with a range of cheeses all selected and tasted by the owner, Henry Voy. If you're curious about any types, he'll be happy to give you a taste or tell you what it's like.

Julien 28

73 av. Franklin D Roosevelt
☏ 42 56 19 81
Ⓜ St-Philippe du Roule métro
Open: Sun–Fri 0630–2000; closed Sun in Aug
American Express

You will almost certainly have to queue to buy something at this in-demand bakery, whether you want their delicious baguettes, croissants, cakes and tarts or a pain au chocolat. There is also a small bar serving coffee and snacks in a room at the back.

La Maison de la Truffe 29

19 pl. de la Madeleine
☏ 42 65 53 22
Ⓜ Madeleine métro
Open: Tue–Sat 0900–2100, Mon 0900–2000
American Express

During the winter truffle season, this is the place to come to find the very best fresh black French truffles, while all year round you can also buy preserved truffles, *foie gras*, smoked fish and meats, and a range of wines and liqueurs.

La Maison du Chocolat 30

225 r. du Faubourg St-Honoré
☏ 42 27 39 44
Ⓜ Ternes métro
Open: Tue–Sat 0930–1900; closed late July–mid-Aug
American Express

There are now several branches of this small chain, founded by one of the most highly regarded chocolatiers in Paris, Robert Linxe. His success is an indication of his talent, producing wonderfully flavoured chocolate, including raspberry and arabica coffee.

René de Saint-Ouen 31

111 blvd Haussmann
☏ 42 65 06 25
Ⓜ Miromesnil métro
Open: Mon–Sat 0700–2000; closed July/Aug
No credit cards accepted

This bakery has a personality all of its own and produces little loaves in the shapes of various birds and animals, which would make an unusual present for the right person. Not all is frivolity, though, as he has won countless awards and twice won the annual prize for the right to produce baguettes for the French president.

Business dining

Dining to impress

In Paris you can dine any style, whether romantic, with children (*see pages 56–7*), chic, cheap or one of the most expensive meals you'll ever have in your life. Business diners are especially well catered for, as here are some of the world's top chefs preparing creations that will impress anyone, generally in equally impressive settings.

If you have a particularly sensitive business meeting, many restaurants do have private dining facilities, catering for any number from two upwards, so if there is a particular place you want to try, it is always worth asking about private rooms. Some which do and which are mentioned elsewhere in this guide include **Pharamond** (*see page 67*) and **Lapérouse** (*see pages 41 and 67*), **La Tour d'Argent** (*see page 31*) and **Guy Savoy** (*see page 60*). On a less-exalted level but more fun and surprising are the **Hard Rock Café** (*see pages 57 and 73*), with a VIP lounge, and **Planet Hollywood** (*78 av. des Champs-Elysées; ✆ 53 83 78 27*), with themed movie rooms.

Taillevent (*15 r. Lamennais; ✆ 45 61 12 90; open: Mon–Fri lunch and dinner; closed four weeks in July/Aug; reservations essential; all credit cards accepted;* ❸❸❸)

> **Turbot with capers, lemon and crushed black truffle is one of the seasonal specialities, while roasted cocoa-bean ice cream exemplifies the original desserts.**

oozes style from the very entrance, on past the stone columns and Louis XV furniture and up the grand staircase. If you want to impress, this is the place to do it, and you could show your knowledge of the menu by asking for one of the specialities, *crépinette* of *andouillette* with *foie gras*. The *farandolle* of desserts allows you to sample a range from the menu. The cellar boasts 130,000 bottles of wine, but that does include some inexpensive choices for those whose expense account is limited.

If you and your business companions appreciate inventive cooking in a stylish setting, then book a table at **Les Élysées du**

▲ Taillevent

Vernet (*Hôtel Vernet, 25 r. Vernet; ∅ 44 31 98 98; open: Mon–Fri lunch and dinner; closed late July–Aug, Christmas and New Year; reservations essential; all credit cards accepted;* ❸❸❸). The dining area is airy and light, thanks to the stunning glass roof designed by Eiffel. The Provençal cooking from chef Alain Solivères, who trained with Alain Ducasse at his Michelin three-starred restaurant in Monaco, is innovative … though his Provence extends from the Basque country in the west to southeastern France, and he blends influences and ingredients from the whole area. Turbot with capers, lemon and crushed black truffle is one of the seasonal specialities, while roasted cocoa-bean ice cream exemplifies the original desserts.

Tiles and glass from the late 19th century enhance the décor at **Pharamond** (*24 r. de la Grande-Truanderie; ∅ 42 33 06 72; open: Mon dinner, Tue–Sat lunch and dinner; reservations recommended; all credit cards accepted;* ❸❸). This is a less grand and less expensive option for a business lunch or dinner, but still impressive and certainly unique. *Tripes à la mode de Caen* (which is beef tripe, vegetables and calvados) is a house speciality on the menu all year round.

Lapérouse (*51 quai des Grand-Augustins; ∅ 43 26 68 04; open: Mon–Fri lunch and dinner, Sat dinner; closed Aug; reservations essential; all credit cards accepted;* ❸❸❸) has ten separate function rooms seating from between 2 to 60 people. This means that the staff and kitchen are used to catering in this manner so it is a safe choice for large meetings. You will be dining where such Parisian luminaries as Colette, Émile Zola and Victor Hugo have all supped before you. The chef Guy Krenzer is noted for several dishes, including *quenelles*, *tournedos Rossini* (combining beef and *foie gras*), and, to round off the meal, ask for one of his soufflés, which are outstanding.

Montmartre and Pigalle

This part of the city is home to the sacred and the profane (the Sacré-Coeur church and the sleaze of Pigalle), and is something of a gastronomic desert compared to the rest of Paris. Its numerous tourists mean abundant fast-food places and plenty of poor-quality options, so it is doubly important to choose wisely before wining and dining.

MONTMARTRE AND PIGALLE
Restaurants

L'Alsaco ❶

10 r. Condorcet

⌀ 45 26 44 31

Ⓟ Poissonnière métro

Open: Mon–Fri lunch and dinner, Sat dinner; closed Aug

Reservations recommended

American Express

French regional

€€

Alsatian cooking tends to be meat-based, hearty and generous, but this friendly little place offers a wider menu showing the best of this French-German cuisine: mutton, beef and potatoes braised in Riesling is one tasty example.

Les Bacchantes ❷

21 r. de Caumartin

⌀ 42 65 25 35

Ⓟ Opéra or Havre-Caumartin métro

Open: Mon–Sat from 1100

Reservations recommended

American Express

French

€€

A simple wine bar, but worth knowing about, in an area short of good eating places. Food ranges from basic salads and charcuterie to more enterprising specials such as duck's neck stuffed with *foie gras*.

Le Cave Drouot ❸

8 r. Drouot

⌀ 47 70 83 38

Ⓟ Richelieu-Druout métro

Open: Mon–Sat from 0630, hot food lunchtime

Reservations recommended

French

€€

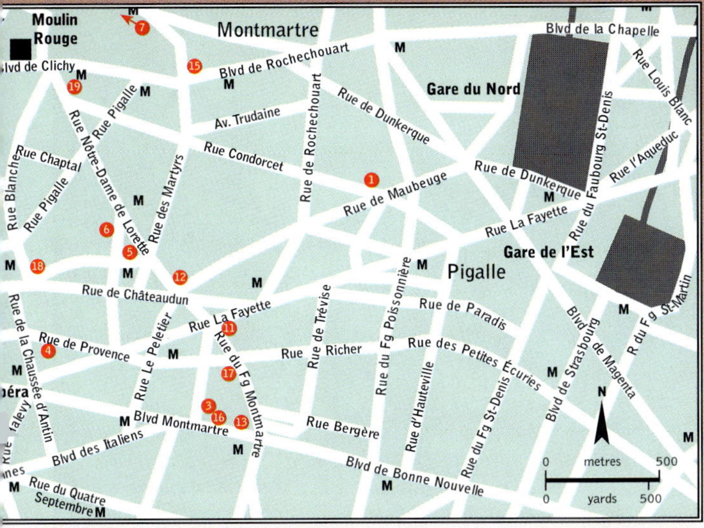

Not many wine bars pay as much attention to food as this one, where you can snack either at the bar, seated in the wine bar, or dine from a larger menu in the restaurant. Steaks, chicken and duck breast are unadventurous but excellently done in generous portions.

Chez Catherine ❹

65 r. de Provence

✆ 45 26 72 88

Ⓜ Chausée d'Antin-La Fayette métro

Open: Mon lunch, Tue–Fri lunch and dinner

Reservations recommended

💳 VISA

French regional

€€

Provençal cooking is the theme at this old-fashioned, relaxed bistro, the kind of place that casual dining in Paris is all about. Tuna steak with mangoes and mushrooms is a contrast to the more traditional meat dishes on offer.

Chez Jean ❺

8 r. St-Lazare

✆ 48 78 62 73

Ⓜ Nôtre-Dame-de-Lorette métro

Open: Mon–Fri lunch and dinner, Sat dinner; closed second week in Aug

Reservations recommended

💳 VISA

French

€€

This excellent little bistro tucked away behind the Galeries Lafayette deserves a mention, and the intimate atmosphere is the perfect accompaniment to excellent food such as red mullet with saffron, served with risotto.

Le Convivial ❻

47 r. St-Georges

✆ 42 85 22 35

Ⓜ St-Georges métro

Open: Mon–Fri lunch and dinner, Sat dinner

Reservations recommended

💳 VISA American Express

French regional

€€

Recipes from Provence influence the menu of

▲ Montmartre

this bistro, whose name hints at the atmosphere they aim at ... and succeed in generating. Sautéed *foie gras* with prunes is just one of the adventurous, and delicious, main courses.

Le Moulin à Vins ❼

6 r. Burq

✆ 42 52 81 27

Ⓜ Abbesses métro

Open: Wed–Thu lunch and dinner, Tue, Fri–Sat dinner; closed Aug

Reservations unnecessary

💳 💳

French

€€

One of the few Montmartre bistros that hasn't sold out to tourism, this is a haven for wine-lovers as the owner adores seeking out interesting wines at reasonable prices. The food sounds simple but is delicious, such as the boeuf bourguignon.

Restaurant Opéra ❽

5 pl. de l'Opéra

✆ 40 07 30 10

Ⓜ Opéra métro

Open: Mon–Fri lunch and dinner; closed part of July/Aug, Christmas and one week in February

Reservations recommended

All credit cards accepted

French

€€€

The magnificent old dining room contrasts with the best of contemporary French cooking which attracts businessmen and diplomats from the surrounding offices, who tuck into dishes such as warm oysters in a brie sauce.

Le Roi du Pot au Feu ❾

34 r. Vignon

✆ 47 42 37 10

Ⓜ Madeleine métro

Open: Mon–Sat from 1200; closed late July–mid-Aug

Reservations recommended

💳 💳 💳

French

€€

The *pot-au-feu* that this bistro claims to be king of is a French staple for Sundays: a stockpot beef stew with potatoes and vegetables. Here it is done to perfection, any day of the week, and while other dishes hold no surprises they are well done and the place is usually busy.

La Verrière [20]

Grand Hôtel Inter-Continental, 2 r. Scribe

⌀ 40 07 32 32

Opéra métro

Open: Mon–Sat lunch and dinner, Sun brunch and dinner; closed Aug

Reservations recommended

All credit cards accepted

French

€€€

This glass-roofed hotel restaurant is filled with light and with plants and caters to hotel guests and visitors alike, but it's not too well known to non-guests. Turbot grilled with sage is a special dish, and wild strawberry and rhubarb pastry make for a tasty dessert.

▲ Sacré-Coeur

MONTMARTRE AND PIGALLE
Bars, cafés and pubs

Au Général Lafayette ⓫

52 r. La Fayette
⌀ 47 70 59 08
Ⓜ Le Peletier métro
Open: daily from 0800, food from 1100
Reservations not allowed
 American Express
€

This unpretentious bar at a drab crossroads welcomes you in with great warmth and it is immediately obvious that most people are regulars. A good range of beers helps wash down simple dishes such as steaks and salads.

Au P'tit Creux du Faubourg ⓬

66 r. du Faubourg Montmartre
⌀ 48 78 20 57
Ⓜ Nôtre-Dame-de-Lorette métro
Open: Mon–Sat from 0730, food lunchtime; closed three weeks in July/Aug
Reservations unnecessary

€

This café-bistro is as ordinary as it gets, which is part of its charm, and if you want a cheap and cheerful meal where the local office workers eat, this is the place. Expect boeuf bourguignon rather than haute cuisine, and a friendly neighbourhood atmosphere.

Café de la Paix ⑧

12 blvd des Capucines
⌀ 40 07 30 20
Ⓜ Opéra métro
Open: daily from 1000, food from 1200
Reservations not allowed
All credit cards accepted
€€

A Parisian café in the grand style, with prices to match, but visitors ought to have a coffee or glass of wine at least once in sumptuous surroundings like this. The food is better elsewhere, but pop your head round the door to soak up the grandeur.

Le Café Zephyr ⓭

12 blvd Montmartre
⌀ 47 70 80 14
Ⓜ Grands Boulevards métro
Open: daily from 0800, food all day
Reservations unnecessary

€€

This off-beat place was founded almost a century ago by people from the Auvergne who loved Algeria, and it maintains the unusual combination of décor and food from both places. You can have just a drink but it would be a shame not to sample the unusual menu.

L'Entract ⓮

1 r. Auber
⌀ 47 42 26 25
Ⓜ Opéra métro
Open: Mon–Sat from 0700, food from 1100
Reservations not allowed
All credit cards accepted
€€

Wood panelling and a great view of the Palais Garnier make the first floor of this old café the place to head for, but a table anywhere means you'll be steeped in history while you sip your coffee or snack on the unadorned meals available.

La Fourmi ⓯

74 r. des Martyrs
⌀ 42 64 70 35
Ⓜ Pigalle métro
Open: Mon–Sat from 0830, Sun from 1030, food 1100–2300
Reservations not allowed
 American Express
€

There are many dubious drinking places around Pigalle, but this is the real thing – complete with long zinc bar. There's basic food available, but most people go for the drinks and the constant busy atmosphere.

Hard Rock Café ⑯
14 blvd Montmartre
∅ 53 24 60 00

🚇 Grands Boulevards métro
Open: daily from 1130
Reservations unnecessary
All credit cards accepted

€€

Like any other Hard Rock Café, but with added Gallic twists, younger travellers might enjoy the change from French cuisine to spare ribs, burgers and milkshakes. There's live music on Thursdays.

Montmartre and Pigalle

MONTMARTRE AND PIGALLE
Shops, markets and picnic sites

Shops

À La Mère de Famille ❶⓻

35 r. du Faubourg Montmartre

⌀ 47 70 83 69

Ⓜ Rue Montmartre métro

Open: Tue–Sat 0830–1330 and 1500–1900; closed Aug

In this homely shop you'll find hundreds of sweets from all over France, as well as the best chocolates, including flavoured ones such as chocolates with blackcurrants and chocolates with raspberry.

▲ The seedy shops in Pigalle

La Bonbonnière de la Trinité [18]

4 pl. d'Estienne d'Orves

∅ 48 74 23 38

⊙ Trinité métro

Open: Mon–Sat 0900–1900; closed Sat in July and Aug

The chocolates produced in this shop are deep and rich, and they make a special chocolate for serving with coffee, as well as selling sweets from the regions of France and a range of homemade jams.

Denise Acabo/À L'Étoile d'Or [19]

30 r. Fontaine

∅ 48 74 59 55

⊙ Blanche métro

Open: Mon–Sat 1030–2000; closed Aug

 American Express

After a while many Parisian chocolate shops do start to look the same, but this one is different. It stocks the best chocolates from all over Paris, whether the maker be in Nice, Paris or in Lyon, where the Bernachon chocolates have been described as the best in the country.

Henri Ceccaldi [20]

21 r. des Mathurins

∅ 47 42 66 52

⊙ Havre-Caumartin métro or Auber RER

Open: Mon–Fri 0830–1930, Sat 1400–1800 (winter only); closed Aug

Corsicans based in Paris stock up in this general food store on all the hearty produce from their native island, including unusual wines (hard to get hold of elsewhere), cheeses, meat, cakes, oils and pastries.

La Maison du Miel [21]

24 r. Vignon

∅ 47 42 26 70

⊙ Madeleine métro

Open: Mon–Sat 0900–1900

The 'House of Honey' is over 100 years old and still sells nothing but honey and honey-based products, such as candles and soap. You can taste any of the many flavours of honey on offer, including unexpected varieties such as chestnut and rhododendron.

Where to eat in the tourist spots

Beware the 'menu touristique'!

One thing any regular traveller knows is that wherever there are tourists, there are people waiting to short-change them, sell them cheap souvenirs, and in the case of restaurants to serve them an indifferent meal because they know the tourists will never come back again anyway. As one of the world's greatest tourist destinations, this applies to Paris just as much as anywhere else. That said, if you chose an eating place at random in Paris you'd be far more likely to have a good meal than by doing the same thing in any other city in the world.

In the busy tourist spots, though, such as the Eiffel Tower and Nôtre-Dame, there are some poor restaurants that cater very much to the passing tourist trade. Beware of the 'menu touristique', on offer at unbelievably cheap prices. The food will probably be poor and it would be a shame to spoil a great visit by rounding it off with a disappointing meal. It's fine if that's what you want, a cheap meal rather than a good one, but if you're planning your day, then think ahead about where you might want to eat, as there are excellent places around all the tourist honey-traps.

At the Eiffel Tower there are two great places actually in the tower itself. On the first floor, aimed at families, is **Altitude 95** (*see page 57*) and on the second floor the more up-market **Jules Verne** (*see page 51*) whose food would warrant an inclusion in any restaurant guide, regardless of the fact that it has some of the finest views in the city.

If visiting the Louvre, try and get into its fashionable café, **Le Café Marly** (*93 r. de Rivoli, cour Napoléon du Louvre; ⌀ 49 26 06 60; open: daily from 0800, hot meals from 1100; reservations not allowed; all credit cards accepted;* ❸). It is situated in the Richelieu wing and has a lovely arcaded section which

▲ The Eiffel Tower

overlooks the courtyard and the stunning glass pyramid, while inside is a plush dining room with velvet armchairs. Dishes are simple, such as salmon tartare, burgers, steaks and salads, with an array of tempting cakes and desserts, but the setting is wonderful and the food well done.

▲ The Louvre

The area around the Sacré-Coeur is one of the worst places in the city for choosing where to eat. There are dozens of options, most of them frequently full as they try to cope with the thousands of visitors who come to see the basilica then wander round the streets of Montmartre to soak up the artistic atmosphere. But which places are filled with tourists and which with more discerning Parisians? For a real Parisian experience just walk down behind Sacré-Coeur itself to the **Aux Négociants** wine bar (*27 r. Lambert; ⌀ 46 06 15 11; open: Mon–Fri from 1200; reservations unnecessary;* VISA; ❶). This unpretentious little place with its ancient zinc bar is a family affair where the husband cooks and waits at table while his wife looks after the bar, always busy with locals. There is only one hot meal, the daily special, which will be something filling and tasty such as leg of lamb with haricot beans simmered in cider, but it will be prepared with care and inexpensive.

> **If you're planning your day, then think ahead about where you might want to eat, as there are excellent places around all the tourist honey-traps.**

If you are arriving in or leaving Paris by Eurostar at the Gare du Nord, you can make your first or last meal a memorable one too. While the station is surrounded by fast-food outlets and has a generally down-at-heel air about it, just five minutes' walk away is the excellent **Chez Michel** (*see page 79*), one of the city's best little restaurants, but you would need to book ahead. If travelling to or from the Gare de Lyon, you don't even need to leave the station to have a memorable dining experience, at **Le Train Bleu** (*Gare de Lyon; ⌀ 43 43 09 06; open: daily lunch and dinner; reservations recommended; all credit cards accepted;* ❶❷❸). Simply walking into the belle-époque interior is an experience in itself, with its chandeliers, painted ceilings, nude statues and comfy leather armchairs. It's a great way to wait for a train, or to celebrate your arrival in the gastronomic capital by tucking into salmon in a red wine sauce or their special veal chops 'Foyot'.

Where to eat in the tourist spots | 77

North and east of the centre

Slightly further out from the main travellers' haunts are some of the best restaurant bargains in the city, thanks to cheap rents and also several of the finest markets in Paris which provide the chefs with excellent fresh produce. You'll also find great cooking from the rest of France, and indeed the rest of the world.

NORTH AND EAST OF THE CENTRE
Restaurants

À Sousceyrac

35 r. Faidherbe
✆ 43 71 65 30
Ⓜ Faidherbe-Chaligny métro
Open: Mon–Fri lunch and dinner, Sat dinner; closed Aug
Reservations recommended
All credit cards accepted
French
€€

This venerable bistro has been here since 1923, but its menu has changed with the times without losing touch with basic dishes. Wild hare stew is one regular, and there is a good wine list too.

Au C'Amelot

50 r. Amelot
✆ 43 55 54 04
Ⓜ Chemin Vert métro
Open: Tue–Sat lunch and dinner; closed Aug
Reservations recommended
⬤ VISA
French
€€

You must be prepared to eat anything to eat in this intimate little place, as the chef prepares a fixed five-course menu each day depending on what he gets fresh from the market. Artichoke soup might be followed by wild boar.

Chez Michel

10 r. Belzunce
✆ 44 53 06 20
Ⓜ Gare du Nord métro
Open: Tue–Sat lunch and dinner; closed for three weeks in Aug and Christmas
Reservations recommended
⬤ VISA
French
€€

Two minutes from the Eurostar terminal, this packed old-fashioned bistro serves exemplary food that belies its appearance. What sounds simple – pork on a bed of cabbage and bacon – is cooked to perfection.

Chez Paul

13 r. de Charonne
✆ 47 00 34 57
Ⓜ Bastille métro
Open: daily lunch and dinner; closed at lunchtime for two weeks in Aug
Reservations recommended
⬤ VISA American Express
French
€€

With its traditional zinc bar and wooden tables, this bistro has been packing them in for decades, locals and tourists alike. The menu is more adventurous than most, with dishes such as rabbit stuffed with goats' cheese and mint.

L'Étoile du Kashmir

63 r. de Charonne
✆ 43 55 57 60
Ⓜ Charonne métro
Open: Tue–Sun lunch and dinner
Reservations unnecessary
⬤ VISA
Indian
€

This inexpensive but pleasant place has several *prix fixe* menus, including one for

▲ L'Étoile du Kashmir

vegetarians, and its dishes range over the entire Indian sub-continent, although they emphasise the use of cardamom in many sauces. Much better fare than the low prices would suggest.

La Galoche d'Aurilliac ❻

41 r. de Lappe
∅ 47 00 77 15
🚇 Bastille métro
Open: Tue–Sat lunch and dinner; closed Aug
Reservations recommended
💳 VISA
French regional
€€

In a street crammed with average eating places, this old-fashioned Auvergne restaurant with a bar at the front is a real treasure. Regional specialities such as stuffed cabbage or sausage are perfectly prepared, and the jovial atmosphere warms the heart.

Les Jumeaux ❼

73 r. Amelot
∅ 43 14 27 00
🚇 Chemin Vert métro
Open: Mon–Fri lunch and dinner, Sat dinner; closed for three weeks in Aug
Reservations recommended
💳 VISA
French
€€

This relaxing restaurant serves up innovative food to match its bright décor. Try scallops on a pea purée with grapefruit butter which is just one example of the chef's experimentation. Daily specials are chalked up on a blackboard that is brought to your table.

Le Villaret ❽

13 r. Ternaux

∅ 43 57 89 76

Ⓜ Parmentier métro

Open: Mon–Fri lunch and dinner, Sat dinner; closed Aug

Reservations recommended

💳 VISA

French

€€

This boisterous restaurant with a bar is usually packed with regulars being greeted warmly, testifying to the quality of the good-value food on offer, with dishes such as venison with mushrooms, chestnuts and cabbage.

La Ville de Jagannath ❾

101 r. St-Maur

∅ 43 55 80 81

Ⓜ St-Maur métro

Open: daily from 1930; closed one week in Aug

Reservations recommended

💳 VISA American Express

Vegetarian-Indian

€€

In a city not overly generous to vegetarians, this *thali* restaurant with its stylish Indian décor is a must – and not just for vegetarians. The menu changes daily depending on the markets, in this ethnically mixed part of Paris, and there are several *prix fixe* menus as well as selections of *thali* dishes available.

La Zygotissoire ❿

101 r. de Charonne

∅ 40 09 93 05

Ⓜ Charonne métro

Open: Mon–Fri lunch and dinner, Sat dinner; closed for two weeks in Aug

Reservations recommended

💳 VISA

French

€

This informal bistro is ideal if you want an inexpensive but very tasty meal in a convivial atmosphere. There is a bargain *prix fixe* menu and the daily specials include such treats as stuffed rabbit roasted on the rotisserie or roasted sea bass.

NORTH AND EAST OF THE CENTRE
Bars, cafés and pubs

L'Armagnac

104 r. de Charonne

✆ 43 71 49 43

Ⓜ Charonne métro

Open: Mon–Fri from 0730, Sat–Sun from 1030

Reservations not allowed

Schizophrenic bar that is an old-fashioned café by day, serving up snacks, coffee and glasses of wine, but at night becomes a young hang-out, with a sound system playing. Choose when you visit, then.

Le Bar Bat

23 r. de Lappe

✆ 43 14 26 06

Ⓜ Bastille métro

Open: daily from 1600, food from 1800

Reservations not allowed

Before or after sampling the rue de Lappe's dining options, this bar with food and a DJ offers a relaxed start to the evening or a frenetic end, or you could pass the whole night away if you weren't fussy about what or where you ate.

Le Baron Bouge

1 r. Théophile-Roussel

✆ 43 43 14 32

Ⓜ Ledru-Rollin métro

Open: Tue–Thu lunchtime and evenings, Fri–Sat 1000–2130, Sun lunchtime, cold snacks all day

Reservations not allowed

Terrific wine bar with upturned barrels on the pavement serving as tables, if you don't mind standing, and a long wine list plus simple tasty snacks, all of which attract an eclectic mix of people from the increasingly fashionable local area. It is also the last wine bar in Paris where you can take along an empty bottle and have it filled from the barrels inside.

Café Charbon ⑭

109 r. Oberkampf

✆ 43 57 55 13

Ⓜ Parmentier métro

Open: daily from 0900, food lunchtime and evenings

Reservations not allowed

The late 19th-century décor of this café/dance hall now resounds to the sounds of loud music every night, though during the day you might be able to enjoy the surroundings rather more peacefully over a drink.

Le Café du Passage ⑮

12 r. de Charonne

✆ 49 29 97 64

Ⓜ Bastille métro

Open: Sat from 1200, Sun–Fri from 1800, food all day

Reservations unnecessary

A wine bar for the serious imbiber, with many

rare vintages as well as examples from less familiar French regions, such as Corsica. The décor is plush, there are regular wine-tastings, and the accompanying food is equally serious in intent: poached egg in a mushroom cream sauce, for example.

Clown Bar

114 r. Amelot
∅ 43 55 87 35
Ⓜ Filles du Calvaire métro
Open: Mon–Sat lunchtime and evenings, Sun evenings only closed one week in Aug
Reservations not allowed

Right by the Cirque d'Hiver, the circus is naturally the theme of this terrific bar, with posters, tiles and memorabilia, not to mention the occasional real clown who might wander in, in full make-up, for a drink between shows.

Jacques Mélac

42 r. Léon-Frot
∅ 43 70 59 27
Ⓜ Charonne métro
Open: Mon–Sat from 0900, hot food lunchtime and evenings but snacks all day; closed two weeks in Aug
Reservations not allowed

Characterful wine bar run by an extravagantly-moustached owner from the Auvergne, who has his own vine on the premises and loves wine deeply. His enthusiasm infects his staff and customers so that the visiting traveller feels welcomed into the family. A sign on the wall informs you that 'Water is reserved for cooking potatoes'.

Le Mecano Bar

99 r. Oberkampf
∅ 40 21 35 28
Ⓜ Parmentier métro
Open: daily from 0900, food lunchtime and evenings
Reservations not allowed
American Express

Definitely unique, this bar done up as a garage workshop offers loud music and inexpensive beers, wine and cocktails, as well as hot meals for lunch and in the evening and cold snacks in between times ... though more as fuel than a culinary experience.

Le Passage

18 passage de la Bonne-Graine
∅ 47 00 73 30
Ⓜ Ledru-Rollin métro
Open: Mon–Fri lunch and dinner, Sat dinner
Reservations recommended
American Express

This mix of wine bar and bistro down a back street near the Bastille has a vast wine list, as well as an extensive menu with the house speciality being a range of *andouillettes*, those spicy sausages that some people find delicious and others disgusting.

NORTH AND EAST OF THE CENTRE
Shops, markets and picnic sites

Shops

À La Petite Fabrique [20]

12 r. St-Sabin

∅ 48 05 82 02

Ⓜ Bastille métro

Open: Tue–Sat 1030–1930

The difference with this chocolate shop is not the choice on offer, which is similar to dozens of other such shops (i.e. wonderful!), but that you can see the chocolates being made in an unbelievably tiny area at the back of the shop. If you ever wondered how they put the brandy into a brandy truffle, this is your chance to find out.

Bazin [21]

85 bis r. de Charenton

∅ 43 07 75 21

Ⓜ Reuilly-Diderot métro

Open: Fri–Tue 0700–2030; closed one week in Feb and part of July or Aug

No credit cards accepted

Close by the Aligre markets, this venerable bakery looks great and smells even better. Here's your chance to try some of Jacques Bazin's unusual creations, such as rye bread baked with almonds, hazelnuts, walnuts and raisins, or one of his organic loaves and rolls.

Le Pain au Naturel [22]

5 pl. d'Aligre

∅ 43 45 46 60

Ⓜ Ledru-Rollin or Faidherbe-Chaligny métro

Open: Tue–Sat 0800–1330 and 1530–2000, Sun 0800–1400

No credit cards accepted

This bakery opened in 1997 in the heart of the Aligre markets with the express intention of

▲ Aligre markets

▲ Richard-Lenoir Market

making only organic breads, but organic does not mean boring. Try the bread with basil or with dried apricots, but be prepared to queue, especially when the market is open.

Le Petit Bleu ㉓

21 r. Jean-Pierre Timbaud
✆ 47 00 90 73
Ⓜ Oberkampf métro
Open: Tue–Sat 1030–2000, Mon 1200–2000; closed two weeks in Aug

From the outside this cheerful shop looks as though it only sells wine, but inside there is an array of other items to interest the food lover, including ceramics, wineglasses, candles, olive oils and sweets. The range of wines is not vast, but it is good, from the inexpensive to the vintage.

Markets

Aligre markets ㉔

Pl. d'Aligre
Ⓜ Ledru-Rollin métro
Open: daily am only

Three markets in one, in and around the place d'Aligre, with a covered market selling the highest quality foodstuffs, where local chefs stock up, and two outdoor markets, one full of junk/antiques, the other of cheaper fruit and vegetables, mostly sold by traders from North Africa.

Popincourt Market ㉕

Blvd Richard-Lenoir near junction with rue Oberkampf
Ⓜ Oberkampf métro
Open: Thu and Sat

This small but lively market, mostly selling foodstuffs, brings in farmers from all around Paris to sell their own produce, so there are some stalls selling a range of fruit and vegetables, while fishmongers and butchers also have their own stalls (*see page 26*).

Richard-Lenoir Market ㉖

Bastille end of blvd Richard-Lenoir
Ⓜ Bastille métro
Open: Thu and Sun

This excellent market sells mainly produce, and anyone visiting Paris for a weekend may want to visit the Sunday morning one to stock up on bits to take home. There are stalls specialising in cheese, bread, honey, wine, mushrooms and many other foodstuffs too.

Paris and wine

Reviving tradition

Paris is more noted these days for serving wine than for making it, although the tradition does cling on in amongst the city streets. One David among the Goliaths of the French wine industry is wine-bar owner **Jacques Mélac** (*see page 83*). Mélac actually has a vine growing in his bar, and he encourages friends, friends of friends, customers and anyone he can think of to grow vines in their gardens, on their balconies and even in a humble window box. There are currently 120 members of his **Association des Vignerons de Paris**, who in the autumn pool their grapes and produce their own vintage – a splendid custom and one which you feel could only happen in Paris. The grapes are of many different varieties, so the wine can be very variable, but that is all part of the fun.

The biggest wine production takes place in **Montmartre**, where there is still a small vineyard behind the Sacré-Coeur along the rue des Saules. It cannot be visited but it is easy to see the 2000 vines through the nets which stop the Parisian birds from sabotaging the city's only sizeable wine harvest. There are several different types of grape grown here, including Gamay and Pinot Noir and there is usually sufficient to make 1000 bottles, which are all sold in aid of charity at 300 francs a bottle. The wine is greeted with great enthusiasm and celebrations when it is produced and sold on the first Saturday in October. The quality doesn't justify the price, but the accompanying street party does.

Wine has been made in Montmartre – though not at this vineyard – for centuries, and indeed it was once a major wine centre whose production was said to match the quality of areas such as Bordeaux and Burgundy. In the mid-18th century there were 20,000 hectares of vineyards in Paris, but after the Industrial Revolution when the population of Paris exploded, the vineyards

were replaced by wheat fields to feed the people, which is why the **Moulin Rouge** (the 'Red Windmill') is in Montmartre. By the late 19th century the vines had gone completely, but the present vineyard was planted in 1933, when a local artist, Francis Poulbot, decided that it was time Montmartre had its vines again.

There are other intriguing wine stories in Paris, including that of two Englishmen, Mark Williamson and Tim Johnston, who took the audacious step of coming to Paris and opening a wine bar. Not only did **Willi's Wine Bar** (*see page 13*) survive, it thrived and has become one of the most popular and fashionable in Paris. There are over 300 French wines available, while at the other wine bar opened later by the same two Englishmen, **Juveniles** (*see page 13*), a range of wines from all over the globe is on offer. This was another bold but successful move in a city whose inhabitants tend to think that good wine doesn't exist beyond the French borders.

Another wine enthusiast is François Clerc, owner of the bistro **Les Bouchons de François Clerc** (*12 r. de l'Hôtel-Colbert; ✆ 43 54 15 34; open: Mon–Fri lunch and dinner, Sat dinner; reservations recommended;* 🔲 🔲 *American Express;* ❷❷). He sells the wines on his excellent wine list at cost, a brave move as heavy wine mark-ups make a great contribution to a typical restaurant's profits. As a result, the place is often booked well ahead, because in addition to the wine bargains, the food is good too! Dishes might include a *croustillant de rouget* (red mullet wrapped in pastry) or sardines pan-fried and then marinated in a mixture of herbs, wine and vinegar. Parisian diners wouldn't come to a place just because the wine is cheap, so the continued success of the Bouchons shows that the food's also worth writing home about.

> **He encourages anyone he can think of to grow vines in their gardens, on their balconies and even in a humble window box.**

Food etiquette and culture

WHERE TO EAT

Parisians tend to eat slightly later than Northern Europeans and North Americans, but not quite as late as in countries further south such as Spain, Greece and Italy. Lunch will be taken at about 1300 to 1400, and it is not uncommon in this city of gastronomy for people to have both a good lunch and a good dinner. Dinner will be eaten from about 2000 or 2030 onwards, so your best bet if you want to dine in a popular place is to turn up, or try to book for, slightly earlier in the evening. But you can eat any time of the day in Paris, as many brasseries serve food from breakfast through till midnight.

The worst days to eat are Sunday and, to a lesser extent, Monday, as many places close on one or other – and sometimes both – of these days. Other restaurants which cater to the business lunchers will not open on Saturday or Sunday. You won't go hungry in Paris but check the opening times in this guide carefully and don't assume that anywhere is automatically open seven days a week. Remember too that many eating places close for at least two weeks during August, when Parisians traditionally take their holidays.

BOOKING AHEAD

The listings in this book say whether booking is recommended in particular restaurants, but of course this is not an infallible guide. When asked by the author if it was essential to book at his restaurant, one of the city's top chefs, Guy Savoy, said, 'People think so but it is not always necessary. We may be booked up a few weeks ahead but we often have late cancellations so it is always worth telephoning to ask.'

The very top places usually require booking weeks, if not months, ahead, especially for evenings at the weekend, but you may be more successful if you're prepared to be flexible and dine at lunchtime during the week. Paris is also a place of fashion, and the latest 'in' place is sure to be booked up well ahead. Even if booking is said to be not necessary, you might still want to telephone the day before to reserve a table, to be on the safe side. Most restaurant staff will speak some English, if you telephone. For a popular,

up-market restaurant, you may also be asked to confirm the table again on the day of the booking, though in most cases this won't be necessary.

DRESS CODE
Only in the top restaurants will men be expected to wear a jacket and tie, but in most other places the 'smart-casual' look is acceptable. However, Paris is Paris, and while you won't be turned away if you don't dress like a fashion model, many diners do dress sharply, and so the scruffy look will probably be decidedly out of place.

COMMON COURTESIES
In all aspects of French life, not just dining, it is important to observe the common courtesies. If greeting someone, whether a friend or a waiter, you must say '*bonjour*' to them during the day and '*bonsoir*' if it is the evening. To launch into conversation, or to ask for a table, without this brief exchange first is considered rude. You will often be greeted in this way by a barman or waiter when entering an establishment and it is important to return the greeting.

WAITING AT TABLE
In Paris the job of waiter or waitress is an honourable and skilled occupation. Generally they do not behave with either the servile or offhand nature of staff in British restaurants, or the over-familiarity commonly seen in North America. There are always exceptions, of course, especially when places are busy, but by and large you will be

served efficiently and in a matter-of-fact manner. The city's reputation for having rude waiters probably comes from a few isolated experiences, and from diners who expect the staff to either act as their best friends or with fawning servility.

SMOKING
Parisians smoke a great deal, even in restaurants, and it is not uncommon to see people smoking before, after and even during courses. All eating establishments must by law have a non-smoking area, but this is often more of a token gesture and may be just a few tables right next to the smoking area. There is little to do but grin and bear it.

TIPPING
Under French law, all bills in cafés and restaurants must include a service charge of about 12 to 15 per cent, so there is no need to add anything to your payment. However, it is also customary to leave a small note, say 10 to 20 francs, for the waiter or waitress if the service has been satisfactory.

Menu decoder

MEALS
le casse-croûte – snack
le déjeuner – lunch
le dîner – dinner
le petit déjeuner – breakfast
le souper – supper

COOKING METHODS
brouillé – scrambled
brûlé(e) – caramelised by burning
à cheval – served with an egg on top
confit – preserved
en croûte – in a pastry case
la daube – meat braised slowly in red wine
au four – oven-baked
fourrée – stuffed/filled
frit(e) – fried
fumé(e) – smoked
gratiné(e) – covered in browned breadcrumbs or cheese
grillé(e) – grilled
haché(e) – chopped or minced
mariné(e) – marinated
meunière – fish, usually sole, that has been seasoned, dusted with flour and fried in butter
minute – fried quickly, as in a minute steak
poché(e) – poached
poêlé(e) – pan-fried
la quenelle – poached dumpling, almost always with pike
le rôti – roast

DRESSINGS
l'aïoli – garlic sauce
l'albert – horseradish sauce
le beurre blanc – butter sauce with white wine, vinegar, cream and shallots
le beurre rouge – butter sauce with red wine
le beurre vert – butter and herb sauce
bordelaise – red wine, shallot and marrow sauce
le chasseur – white wine, mushroom, shallot and tomato sauce
la crème anglaise – custard
florentine – cooked/served with spinach/spinach sauce
le moutard – mustard
le pistou – basil and garlic sauce, like the Italian pesto
la poivrade – pepper sauce served with meat dishes

FISH AND SEAFOOD
l'aiglefin – haddock
l'anchois – anchovy
le bar – sea bass
la bouillabaisse – fish and shellfish soup
la bourride – fish stew
le brochet – pike
le bulot – whelk
le cabillaud – fresh cod
le calamar – squid
le carrelet – plaice
le chipiron – squid
les coquillages – shellfish
la coquille St-Jacques – scallops
la crevette – prawn/shrimp
le crustacé – crustaceans/shellfish
la darne – fish steak
la daurade/dorade – sea bream
l'éperian – whitebait
l'espadon – swordfish
le flétan – halibut
les fruits de mer – seafood
le hareng – herring

le homard – lobster
l'huître – oyster
la langoustine – Dublin Bay prawn/scampi
la limande – lemon sole
la lisette – small mackerel
la lotte – monkfish
le maquereau – mackerel
le merlu – hake
la morue – salt cod
les moules – mussels
le poisson – fish
le poulpe – octopus
le rouget – red mullet
St-Pierre – John Dory
le sandre – pikeperch
le saumon – salmon
le thon – tuna
la truite – trout

MEAT DISHES
les abats – offal
l'agneau – lamb
l'aiguillette – top rump of beef
l'aloyau – loin of beef
l'andouillette – grilled sausage made from offal
la bavette – steak from beef flank
la biche – deer/venison
le bifteck – beefsteak
le blanc de poulet – chicken breast
le boeuf – beef
le boeuf gros sel – boiled beef with vegetables
le boudin blanc – white sausage (veal, pork or chicken)
le boudin noir – black pudding
la brochette – kebab
le canard – duck
la carbonnade – beef stew with beer and onions
le carré d'agneau – rack or loin of lamb
le cassoulet – duck, sausage and bean stew
la cervelle – brains
la charcuterie – cold and cured meats, such as ham and pâté, often served as a mixed plate
chateaubriand – fillet steak
le cheval – horse
la choucroute garnie – sauerkraut topped with ham and sausages
le civet – game stew in a sauce thickened with blood
le cochon – pig
le contre-filet – sirloin steak
la cuisse – leg of poultry
la dinde – turkey
l'entrecôte – beef rib steak
l'escalope – cutlet
l'estouffade – meat stew
le faux-filet – sirloin steak
le filet mignon – tenderloin
le foie gras – fattened goose or duck liver
la fricadelle – meatball
le gibier – game
le gigot d'agneau – leg of lamb
le jambon – ham
le lapin – rabbit
le lard – bacon
le lièvre – hare

le mouton – mutton
l'oie – goose
le porc – pork
le poulet – chicken
la queue de boeuf – oxtail
le ragoût – meat stew
le rognon – kidney
le rosbif – roast beef
le rumsteck – rumpsteak
le sanglier – wild boar
le saucisson – small sausage
les travers de porc – spare ribs
le veau – veal
la viande – meat
la volaille – poultry

HERBS, NUTS, PULSES AND VEGETABLES
l'ail – garlic
l'artichaut – artichoke
l'asperge – asparagus
l'aubergine – aubergine/eggplant
le basilic – basil
le céleri – celery
le champignon – mushroom
la chiffonade – shredded herbs and vegetables
le chou – cabbage
le chou-fleur – cauliflower
la choucroute – sauerkraut
le concombre – cucumber
la courge – squash/vegetable marrow
la courgette – courgette/zucchini
les crudités – raw vegetables
les épices – spices
les épinards – spinach
les fines herbes – mixed herbs
la girolle – wild mushroom
le haricot vert – green bean
la laitue – lettuce
le légume – vegetable
la lentille – lentil
le marron – chestnut
la menthe – mint
l'oignon – onion
le panais – parsnip

le persil – parsley
le petit pois – pea
le piment – pepper/chilli pepper
le poireau – leek
la pomme de terre – potato
le radis – radish
le riz – rice
la roquette – rocket
le safran – saffron
la sauge – sage
le thym – thyme
la truffe – truffles

FRUIT
l'abricot – apricot
les agrumes – citrus fruits
l'airelle – cranberry
l'ananas – pineapple
l'avocat – avocado
le cassis – blackcurrant
la cerise – cherry
le citron – lemon
le citron vert – lime
la citrouille – pumpkin
le coing – quince
la datte – date
la figue – fig
la fraise – strawberry
la framboise – raspberry
le genièvre – juniper berry
la grenade – pomegranate
la griotte – morello cherry
la groseille – redcurrant
la groseille à maquereau – gooseberry
le litchi – lychee
la mangue – mango
la mirabelle – small yellow plum
la mûre – blackberry
le pamplemousse – grapefruit
la pastèque – watermelon
la poire – pear
la pomme – apple
la prune – plum
le pruneau – prune
le raisin – grape
la tomate – tomato

DESSERTS AND CHEESE
le bavarois – a cream dessert
la brebis – a sheeps' milk cheese
la charlotte – type of cream dessert in buttered bread mould usually filled with fruit, apple charlotte, for example
le chèvre – goats' cheese
le chocolat – chocolate
la crème brûlée – cream dessert with caramelised top
le crottin – small, round goats' cheese
la florentine – toffee and nut biscuit covered in chocolate (*see also Dressings*)
le fondant – type of chocolate dessert
le fromage – cheese
le fromage blanc – cream cheese
le gâteau – cake
la glace – ice cream or just ice
la tarte Tatin – apple tart served upside down with caramel

DRINKS
l'abricotine – apricot brandy
les alcools – spirits
la bière – beer
la bière blanche – light lager beer
la bière brune – dark beer
blanc – white
la boisson – a drink
le café – coffee (usually a small espresso)
le café au lait – coffee with milk
le café grand – large coffee
le calvados – apple brandy
le cardinal – kir made with red wine
le cassis – blackcurrant liqueur used in kir
le chocolat chaud – hot chocolate
le citron pressé – freshly squeezed lemon juice
décaffeiné – decaffeinated
doux/douce – sweet
de l'eau – water
l'écrémé – skimmed milk
gazeuze – fizzy, as in bottled water
l'infusion – herbal tea
le jus de fruits – fruit juice
le kir – white wine mixed with blackcurrant liqueur
le kir royale – kir made with champagne
du lait – milk
la limonade – lemonade
la mirabelle – plum brandy
l'orange pressée – freshly squeezed orange juice
le pichet – carafe/jug, of water or wine
le plat(e) – still or non-fizzy water
la poire Williams – pear brandy
le porto – port
rosé – rosé
rouge – red
sec – dry
du thé – tea
la tisane – herbal tea
la verre – glass
la vieille prune – plum brandy
du vin – white
le vin du table – table wine
l'xérès – sherry

Menu decoder | 93

Recipes

Parisian cooking is primarily traditional French cooking with many influences from the different French regions, each with their own strong cuisine, especially areas such as Normandy, Provence or the Auvergne. There is therefore very little that can be said to be authentically Parisian, but of course it would be hard to return home without wanting to make at least one rich chocolate dish of some kind, perhaps with chocolate bought in Paris. *Salade niçoise* is a Parisian bistro favourite, regardless of its origins, and a good example can be a meal in itself.

Chocolate cake

Serves 8–10

INGREDIENTS

300g of rich chocolate, such as Lindt
100g sugar
200g unsalted butter
5 eggs, separated
salt

Break the chocolate into pieces and melt over simmering water. When melted, add and stir in thoroughly 70g of the sugar, then add and stir all the butter, and finally the egg yolks. The ingredients should be thoroughly mixed.

Beat the egg whites with a pinch of salt until they are stiff, then add the rest of the sugar and beat till the mixture turns glossy.

Take the chocolate mix off the heat and add one-third of the egg white mixture, folding gently but blending thoroughly with the chocolate. Then do the same with the remaining two-thirds of the mixture.

Dampen a springform pan and fill it with the chocolate mix while it is still wet. Place in the refrigerator for 24 hours, and remove 30 minutes before serving. Serve on its own, or with cream or a vanilla ice cream, or perhaps with an apricot sauce.

Salade niçoise

Serves 4

INGREDIENTS

the leaves from the heart of a crisp lettuce

6 tomatoes, quartered

3 hard-boiled eggs, quartered

450g of tinned tuna, flaked

4 anchovy fillets, washed

16 black olives, de-stoned and roughly cut

The dressing:

4 tbsp of virgin olive oil

1 tbsp of wine vinegar

1 clove of garlic

1 teaspoon of capers, washed

2 tbsp of chopped fresh parsley

salt

pepper

Individual servings look better and are easier to eat so take four small salad bowls and line them with the lettuce leaves. Add the tomatoes, eggs and tuna.

Prepare the dressing, then dress and gently toss the salad before placing the anchovy fillets on top and finally scattering in the olives.

Published by Thomas Cook Publishing
Thomas Cook Holdings Ltd
PO Box 227
Thorpe Wood
Peterborough PE3 6PU
United Kingdom

Telephone: 01733 503571
Email: books@thomascook.com

Text © 2001 Thomas Cook Publishing
Maps © 2001 Thomas Cook Publishing

ISBN 1 841570 58 3

Distributed in the United States of America by the Globe Pequot Press, PO Box 480, Guilford, Connecticut 06437, USA

Publisher: Donald Greig
Commissioning Editor: Deborah Parker
Map Editor: Bernard Horton

Project management: Dial House Publishing
Series Editor: Christopher Catling
Copy Editor: Lucy Thomson
Proofreader: Jan Wiltshire

Series and cover design: WhiteLight
Cover artwork: WhiteLight and Kaarin Wall
Text layout: SJM Design Consultancy, Dial House Publishing
Maps prepared by Polly Senior Cartography

Repro and image setting: PDQ Digital Media Solutions Ltd
Printed and bound in Italy by Eurografica SpA

Written and researched by: **Mike Gerrard**

The author would like to say thank you to *Eurostar* for getting him to Paris; to Room Service (∅ *070 2636 6888*) and the Hotel Plessis for a wonderful stay; and to Alain Ducasse for the best meal he's ever had in his life.

We would like to thank the author for the photographs used in this book, to whom the copyright belongs, with the exception of the following:
Donna Dailey (pages 2, 7, 21, 22, 35B, 45, 57, 83, 84, 85, 91 and 93)
Chris Fairclough (pages 39, 40, 42, 50, 53, 56, 70, 71, 73, 74, 76, 77 and 89)
P. Hussenot (page 10)
Caroline Jones (page 31)
Guy Savoy (page 60)
Neil Setchfield (pages 3 and 95)
Edith Summerhayes (page 94).

All rights reserved. No part of this publication may be reproduced, stored in a retrieval system or transmitted, in any form or by any means, without the prior permission of the publishers.

The contents of this book are believed to be correct at the time of printing. Establishments may open, close or change and Thomas Cook Holdings Ltd cannot accept responsibility for errors or omissions, or for the consequences of any reliance on the information provided. Descriptions and assessments are given in good faith but are based on the authors' views and experience at the time of writing and therefore contain an element of subjective opinion which may not accord with the reader's subsequent experiences. The opinions in this book do not necessarily represent those of Thomas Cook Holdings Ltd.